RETIREMENT
BLUEPRINT

The first steps to building
a better lifestyle in retirement

ED DOWNEY

Ed Downey/Downey Financial Group
806 W. Bartlett Road, Bartlett, IL 60103
www.downeyfg.com

Book layout ©2022 Advisors Excel, LLC

Retirement Blueprint/Ed Downey — 1st edition

ISBN 9798842753161

"Money is only a tool. It will take you wherever you wish, but it will not replace you as the driver."

~ Ayn Rand

This book is dedicated to my dad, Ed Sr., and Uncle Marty. Without them, there would be no Downey Financial Group or book. The friendship they had with each other and the kindness they showed their employees was a model for how I wanted to run my professional life. Their clients loved them and it was easy to see why. They took me in and taught me a wonderful craft. Thank you, Dad and Uncle Marty.

Table of Contents

The Importance of Planning

I grew up in a house where no one planned for anything. More effort went into deciding where we were going to spend a long Memorial Day weekend than any conversations we had about college, careers, or money. This was a little surprising in retrospect, as my dad did planning for a living. He was an estate planning attorney.

I was born and raised in the south part of Chicago in a time before cellphones, video games, or social media. A good day meant we had a long game of "kick the can," or massive hide-and-seek games that encompassed an entire Chicago city block.

My dad, Ed Sr., was an attorney who owned his own small practice with an estate planning focus (I am technically Ed Jr., but I don't use the Jr. part too much). His office was at 103rd and Western Avenue in the Beverly neighborhood of Chicago. It was a great place to see the famous South Side St. Patrick's Day Parade every year!

Dad was a good listener. He also had a great capacity for empathy. The combination of these two things made him a real rarity: a likable attorney. So many of my dad's old clients have told me how lucky I am to have a great father like him. I totally agree. I bet not too many children of attorneys ever heard anything like that from their dad's clients!

Across the hall from my dad's Beverly office was the office of my Uncle Marty. Uncle Marty was a CPA who also had his own practice specializing in helping individual families and their small businesses. Uncle Marty and Dad worked as a team, with Uncle Marty doing the tax planning and preparation, and then Dad doing the family legal work. When I got into the financial services business in 1992, Dad and Uncle Marty brought me in to help many of their combined clients. So, I was kind of baptized into a culture of having sound tax planning, legal planning, and financial planning all synced together. The professionals in those three areas all communicate with each other and build suggestions based on all three areas. Dad and I ended up working closely together all my adult life. Dad referred me to many of my first clients.

Early in my financial planning career, my parents got a divorce. This was not a big shock to me or my siblings. We knew they were both good people, just not good for each other. Now I was a still pretty immature twenty-four-year-old, and I did not really understand fully what this would mean for my mom and dad financially, but as I would find out, it was not good. Especially for Mom.

My mom, Eileen, was a stay-at-home mom. She quit her teaching career in 1968 when I was born. She had to fight to get back into the workforce after the divorce. Even though she had a master's in teaching, she had to go back to college and redo several classes to reinstate her teaching license. But she did it. She was a tough, fighting lady.

Mom was able to get a job back with the same school district she worked for in 1968. She really loved teaching and made a lot of new friends at her school. I would come by and take her to lunch occasionally, and the other teachers would always comment on how lucky I was to have a funny mom like Eileen. I was lucky. Mom was really the first one who exposed me to investing and the stock market. She loved to purchase penny stocks and dreamed of seeing one of them become the next Microsoft. But that never happened.

A couple of years into my financial planning career, Mom confided in me that although her day-to-day financial situation had stabilized since the divorce, she had some real concerns about her retirement. It was very evident to me she was in real trouble. She had a minimal pension coming, her Social Security, and the money she had from the divorce settlement. It was a good amount of money. She got more from the divorce settlement than Dad, but was it enough? Eileen was already sixty-three at this point and retirement was approaching quickly. Knowing my mom's lifestyle needs, it was easy for me to see: Eileen was going to run out of money in retirement, and probably early. The amount of money she was living on as a teacher was going to be very difficult to duplicate.

I felt so helpless. Really, there was little I could do. There were just a handful of years between that point and when Mom would need to start taking significant withdrawals out of her savings. Putting the money in the stock market might help the money last longer, OR it could make her run out of money even faster if we had a market crash—and that is probably what would happen.

And then a miracle happened: My mom's school district allowed her to take a big chunk of her divorce settlement and buy back into her teacher's pension as if she had worked all those years since 1968! It totally saved her retirement and her lifestyle. It was also just sheer luck. If it wasn't for that little miracle, my mom's retirement years would have been financially bleak.

What I learned from that experience is that although Mom saw this coming a mile away, she did not plan for it. She was just hoping everything would work out okay. I am not anti-hope, but hope is not a plan. As I grew in my financial planning career, I learned that Mom's situation was fixable even without that little miracle. The earlier we would have gotten started on the planning, the more effective I could have been, but I believe her situation was fixable. So, I became passionate about planning.

Simplifying the Planning Process

I believe most people think the most important thing they need for retirement is a bunch of money, or investments providing exceptional rates of return. Or maybe they think they just need to make more money at work so they can save more, or have the investment advisor with the best TV show, or some other magic bullet solution. Well, I have some good news for you if that is what you believe: it is just not that difficult!

What you need more than anything is to organize what you already have going on so far for retirement, get clarity on what you are going to need for your lifestyle income, and then let that dictate course corrections you need to make now to give you the highest probability of success. That is what a retirement income and tax plan truly is. We call our retirement income and tax planning process the Retirement Blueprint.

I know you read this and think that it sounds complicated. Especially figuring out what your lifestyle income needs are not only today, but ten years from now, twenty years from now, and so on. Well, that is one of the beautiful things about having a written retirement income and tax plan. The tools are out there to help you quantify all those things. Our Retirement Blueprint process has been streamlined over thirty years to help our clients make this process as easy and understandable as possible.

Many of my clients have stated that for the first time, they have true clarity on what they have and what they need to do for retirement. Although I believe the process will be smoother and the results more reliable if you work with a professional, this type of planning is something you can start to do for yourself. Therein lies the purpose of this book.

Some expenses in retirement will happen for sure. You are going to continue to buy groceries, buy gasoline, have a cellphone and utilities, and so on. The good news is those are expenses you can look up easily in your current lifestyle expenses today. If some of them are annual payments, break them down to a monthly average. I also find these represent the majority of what my clients' lifestyle expenses are—more good news for getting this chore done.

But some of your monthly lifestyle expenses are a little bit more subjective. These are also the most important. They are items like: How much do you spend on travel? Do you think you will travel more in retirement? If you have family that no longer live in the area, will you be traveling to visit them more? Do you give to church or charity? Do you think that will increase or decrease in retirement? Do you purchase a new car every few years, or do you drive them until they fall apart? Do you intend on purchasing a second home in retirement or a vacation home? Do you think you will spend more on activities like golf, fishing, or sporting in retirement? Do you intend on starting that small business you always wanted to? How much will that cost?

Although those may sound hard to answer, everything above has an answer and is able to be converted into a monthly average dollar amount. We call it "quantifying" your monthly lifestyle income. Not only the expenses you have today, but the expenses that will start down the road (like Medicare Supplements or out-of-pocket medical expenses). Once you have them written down, you need to apply an average inflation rate to start to forecast what type of income you're going to need in ten years, twenty years, and the rest of your life.

You are absolutely, positively, 100 percent going to have expenses down the road, and they are more predictable than you think. Now is the time to get an idea of what they might be. This is what I am talking about when I refer to getting clarity on where you are right now and where you are heading.

A great analogy would be if you were going to go on a cross-country road trip. The first thing you would need to know is, where am I on the map right now? Second would be, where am I trying to get to on the map? Imagine if you just pulled out of the driveway and started driving and didn't really give any thought to where you were going until you were about twelve hours down the road. How do you think your trip would go? When was the time to figure out where it was that you were trying to go? Figuring out your monthly lifestyle expenses today is the equivalent of finding out where you are on the financial map, and the first step of discovering where you want to go.

Most people do not complete a written retirement income and tax plan because they think it's just too difficult. In many cases, they don't even start. Whatever happens, happens. Hopefully, it's not a disaster. The reality is the process is not nearly as difficult as most people think. This is where working with a professional can be very important. Having someone who can walk you through all the organizational items needed to find out where you are on the financial map, where you are trying to go, and then go over suitable suggestions for improvement in a format that is easy to understand can be extremely powerful.

Like figuring out those subjective lifestyle expenses, for instance. I find that individuals who do planning on their own tend to cheat themselves a bit, only including survival-type items and not including the things that really make life worth living. In many cases, I act as a bit of a coach with my clients to help them uncover what their true feelings are about what they want their lifestyle to look like and then turn that into a number. Quantifying. Other times I find people have abandoned the process on their own because they think their situation is hopeless. It is very seldom that I find a potential client's retirement situation hopeless.

Most of the Retirement Blueprint clients we work with not only have confidence that their plan will work, but in many cases, they grow beyond those initial income needs and start adding on additional things like early retirement, vacation homes, or grandchildren's college education funds.

Regardless, with our planning, clients have fewer concerns about money. And that is our main goal.

Taking It One Step at a Time

When we have a new Retirement Blueprint client, the very first step is to help them discover and clarify what is most important to them about this next phase of their life. I think this is what makes us different as well. Most financial advisors start from a mathematical standpoint when working with a new client.

"How much do you have in retirement assets? How much mortgage debt do you have left? How much do you have in stocks, in bonds?"

They start off in many cases with questions like these.

I believe the most important question to ask is: What are you passionate about once you stop working? If we were to meet three years *after* your retirement date, and you were to look *back* over those three years, what would have needed to have happened for you to feel truly happy about your progress?

Retirement isn't about how much money you end up with or what tax bracket you're in. Retirement is about having the lifestyle you have worked so hard for and doing the things you are passionate about. That is what you need to focus on at the beginning. Those goals and dreams can be turned into numbers. We do it all the time. Not only is it where you start, but it should permeate and affect all the other financial decisions that you make.

The problem with not having a written retirement income and tax plan is that in most cases, the individual has no clue if a financial disaster is right around the corner. Their decision process is "from the gut," or because they were sold something by a slick salesperson. Even if their investment structure is good, they are not confident in it because they have no idea if it's pointing them in the direction they really want to go. And that's because the direction hasn't even been figured out yet 100 percent. Maybe their financial structure is sound. Maybe it's not, and they're on a path of running out of money. Maybe their taxes are going to be okay. Maybe their taxes are going to eat up their estate.

Or they just decide to do nothing because they are afraid of making the wrong decision (which, by the way, is still a decision). These folks are even less confident in their financial situation because they know something should have been done, (probably a lot of somethings) but wasn't.

This creates anxiety about retirement.

In many cases, I find people significantly postpone their retirement date, mainly because they are so stressed about whether it will work. Or they live so far below their means that it prevents them from living the lifestyle they really wanted or fulfilling the dream items they have been passionate about all their life. In most cases, I find these clients can have the lifestyle they want; very rarely do I meet a potential client who I just can't help.

I believe this is all fixable by gaining clarity about what it is that you want in retirement and then having a written plan of action to make it happen. A written retirement income and tax plan, in black and white. When you have a written plan like this, all of the guesswork is taken out of the situation. You know what it is you need for your financial lifestyle, you have clarity on what investment choices to consider, and you know what to do to be proactive on taxes.

A good analogy here would be building a house. What would be the first thing you would need to do before you started building your house? Before you bought any wood, conduit, or drywall? Maybe even before you bought the land you were going to build the house on? You would need to hire an architect and start to sketch out a blueprint for your house. Imagine for a moment if you decided not to hire the architect. You just went to Home Depot and started to amass the wood, the conduit, the drywall, and went out to your land and started digging holes and putting posts in the ground. How do you think your house would turn out?

Well, as funny as that sounds, it is more than likely what you've been doing so far for your financial house. You might have gotten away with it during your working years, but it is going to be much more difficult and there will be many more obstacles in the retirement phase.

At the end of the day, I believe that not having a plan creates significant anxiety for people in retirement. It doesn't matter if you are wealthy or middle class. Not knowing which ripple effects your actions or inactions have created will probably keep you up at night. My bet is they'll also keep your spouse up at night as well if you have one. But they might not say anything to you because they think you are the one who has it "all figured out" and that "everything's okay." After all, you are the one reading this book.

Our goal is to help people worry less about money. We state that right on our website. How we do that is by creating a written retirement income and tax Retirement Blueprint plan with our clients and then executing that plan. When you get clarity about what the materials are that you need for your financial house and where they are supposed to go, you make smarter decisions and have much more confidence in the probable outcomes. This is what a Retirement Blueprint does.

In the chapters that follow, we'll cover some of the basic principles and processes we use in our practice to help clients on their path to retirement. But first, let's address some of the common roadblocks you may encounter.

Potential Risks to Your Ideal Retirement

Ever feel like life gets in the way and prevents you from doing things you should not ignore? I think if we're honest with ourselves, we've all put off obligations we know are important.

In your case, you may be reading this book because it's time to get serious about financial planning and, specifically, devising a way to best prepare for retirement. A retirement income plan should be based on more components than just your investments or your finances. The preparation of that strategy begins with your desires, ambitions, and goals for this fulfilling season of life.

There's no such thing as a silly question. Not when one of the most common questions we hear from folks regarding retirement is, "Am I going to be okay?" Often, it seems, people are reluctant to meet with financial professionals because they worry they might sound uneducated. Yet, it's understandable for you to be a

x | ED DOWNEY

novice when it comes to financial issues and retirement concerns. You've been busy with your lives and your careers. Time spent away from work has meant time spent being around those you love and engaging in the activities you enjoy. Retirement provides the opportunity to do even more of that, while not fretting over work obligations.

Concerns people have about what they may encounter during retirement can be far-reaching and still perfectly legitimate. For a quick snapshot, I want to provide a brief sampling of wide-ranging issues that can come up during discussions about what to potentially brace for in retirement. This book will touch on many of these issues in further detail.

Politics: A presidential election often stirs emotions regarding potential effects on the economy. Investors grow anxious about how a new president can influence market returns. It's Congress, however, that establishes tax laws and passes spending bills. Yet the president can indirectly affect the economy and the stock market in various ways such as the appointment of policymakers, development of international relations, and influential sway on new legislation.

Taxes: An example of a president's influence can be cited in signature legislation passed during Donald Trump's presidency, the Tax Cuts and Jobs Act of 2017. However, our tax system remains progressive, so the more you earn, the higher the tax rate within each tax bracket of subsequently higher income. A thorough understanding of tax regulations can be crucial. A financial professional can help identify potential issues a tax professional can help solve.

Inflation: Government spending, which most recently spiked with relief packages designed to assist U.S. citizens during the COVID-19 pandemic, can fuel concerns of inflationary hikes stemming from an influx of money thrust at the same consumer goods. A retiree's income can be impacted by the effect inflation can have on fixed expenses. The value of currency decreases because inflation erodes purchasing power.

Health pandemic: The coronavirus outbreak could impact how Americans view risks and re-examine healthy habits. That, potentially, could be one of the effects of COVID-19 as we assess how long a pandemic can last and if others will occur in our lifetimes. The cost of health care can be surprising throughout retirement. It could become an issue people focus on even more following the pandemic, which had a particularly acute impact on some U.S. elder care facilities.

Cybersecurity: Think you'll give up your smartphone in retirement? No way, right? It's here to stay, along with other intellectual gadgetry, including devices that have not been patented or invented. Retirees are becoming more tech-savvy, yet they can also be more trusting, which can be problematic when responding to potential scammers by phone, text, or email. Cybercrime often uses technology to target potential victims. Scammers, much like technology, figure to only grow more sophisticated over time.

CHAPTER 1

Longevity

You would think the prospect of the grave would loom more frightening as we age, yet many retirees say their number one concern is actually running out of money in their twilight years.[1] This concern is, unfortunately, justified, in part, because of one significant factor: We're living longer.

According to the Social Security Administration's 2011 Trustee Report, in 1950, the average life expectancy for a sixty-five-year-old man was seventy-eight, and the average for a sixty-five-year-old woman was eighty-one. Those averages were expected to be eighty-three and eighty-six, respectively by the year 2021.[2]

The bottom line of many retirees' expense woes comes down to this: They just didn't plan to live so long. Now, when we are younger and in our working years, that's not something we necessarily see as a bad thing; don't some people fantasize about living forever or, at least, reaching the ripe old age of one hundred?

However, with a longer lifespan, as we near retirement, we face a few snags. Our resources are finite—we only have so much

---

[1] Liz Weston. nerdwallet.com. March 25, 2021. "Will You Really Run Out of Money in Retirement?" https://www.nerdwallet.com/article/finance/will-you-really-run-out-of-money-in-retirement
[2] Social Security Administration. 2011 Trustees Report. "Actuarial Publications: Cohort Life Expectancy." https://www.ssa.gov/OACT/TR/2011/lr5a4.html

money to provide income—but our lifespans can be unpredictably long, perhaps longer than our resources allow. Also, longer lives don't necessarily equate with healthier lives. The longer you live, the more money you will likely need to spend on health care, even excluding long-term care needs like nursing homes.

You will also run into inflation. If you don't plan to live another twenty-five years but end up doing so, inflation at an average 3 percent will approximately double the price of goods over that time period. Put a harsh twist on that and the buying power of a ninety-year-old will be half of what they possessed if they retired at sixty-five.[3]

Because we don't necessarily get to have our cake and eat it, too, our collective increased longevity hasn't necessarily increased the healthy years of our lives. Typically, our life-extending care most widely applies to the time in our lives where we will need more care in general. Think of common situations like a pacemaker at eighty-five, or cancer treatment at seventy-eight.

"Wow, Ed," I can hear you say. "Way to start with the good news first."

I know, I've painted a grim picture, but all I'm concerned about here is cost. It's hard to put a dollar sign on life, but that is essentially what we're talking about when discussing longevity and finances. Living longer isn't a bad thing; it just costs more, and one key to a sound retirement strategy is preparing for it in advance.

I have a great example of a client couple who really understood longevity and took advantage of the financial tools available to them. I will call these clients Marty and Ellen.

When I first met Marty and his great wife Ellen, she was already retired, and Marty was getting set to. They both felt good

[3] Bob Sullivan, Benjamin Curry. Forbes. April 28, 2021. "Inflation And Retirement Investments: What You Need to Know."
https://www.forbes.com/advisor/retirement/inflation-retirement-investments

with the income they had coming in from Social Security and a pension. They didn't think they would use too much of their retirement money. In fact, their nest egg was more for emergency "what-if's." One of the most important what-if's on Marty's mind was if he got sick or died early in their retirement. That money would need to go for his care and be there to support Ellen, since his pension would not continue for her 100 percent if he died, and they would lose one of their Social Security payments. That concern was strong enough for Marty that they didn't really use any of their retirement nest egg money and had no plans to. Even though they had dreams of traveling the world and seeing all the sites they always wanted to see, they felt pulling the trigger on that might threaten their financial situation long-term, especially for Ellen.

I also discovered that Marty and Ellen did not have any kind of written retirement income and tax plan. "Why would we need to? Our Social Security and pension income completely covers our lifestyle," was one of the things they said in our introductory meeting. But the more I asked them about what was most important in retirement, they kept coming back to traveling more, if they could afford it.

Marty and Ellen turned into one of my favorite Retirement Blueprint experiences. The hypothetical forecasting capabilities of our program showed there was plenty of capacity for them to start using their nest egg for their travel dreams and still have it be there for the what-if's. Their portfolio just needed to be structured properly to give it the highest probability of success. Marty went so far as to decide to purchase a life insurance policy to act as a backup plan; the premiums were paid by the additional unneeded income from the unused nest egg. By doing that, Marty really made the portfolio bulletproof for Ellen.

So, Marty and Ellen traveled the world. They were my favorite travel guides! My wife, Shannon, and I have visited many of the cities they loved and stayed at several of the hotels they suggested. I often got postcards from exotic locations with fantastic little notes, often with a rating on the hotel (it is tough to get an A from Ellen!).

Sadly, Marty died at age eighty after a three-year battle with cancer. But because of their actions, Ellen was very well set years after. She had significantly more in assets and more in income capabilities than what she needed. She absolutely treasured the ten years of travel memories she had with Marty—but she refused to revisit any of the locations they enjoyed together. The travel planning got a bit tough, as she had been all over the world!

From age eighty-five to eighty-eight, she was more socially active, with many visits from family and friends. She participated in more activities than she had in the seven years since her husband died. Her planning from decades earlier allowed her to pass on a legacy to her children when she passed away herself. The legacy she left behind can be measured both in dollar signs *and* in other intangible ways.

Living longer may be more expensive, but it can be so meaningful when you plan for your "just-in-cases."

Retiring Early

A key part of planning for retirement revolves around retirement income. After all, retirement is cutting the cord that tethers you to your employer—and your monthly check. However, that check often comes with many other benefits, particularly health care. Health care is often the thing that can unexpectedly put dreams for an early retirement on hold. Some employers offer health benefits to their retired workers, but that number has declined drastically over the past several decades. In 1988, among employers who offered health benefits to their workers, 66 percent offered health benefits to their retirees. By 2020, that number had since diminished to 29 percent.[4]

---

[4] Henry J. Kaiser Family Foundation. October 8, 2020. "2020 Employer Health Benefits Survey Section Eleven: Retiree Health Benefits."

So, with employer-offered retirement health benefits on the wane, this becomes a major point of concern for anyone who is looking to retire, particularly those who are looking to retire before age sixty-five, when they would become eligible for Medicare coverage. Fidelity estimates that the average retired couple at age sixty-five will need approximately $300,000 for health care expenses in retirement, not including long-term care.[5] Do you think it's likely that cost will decrease?

Even if you are working until age sixty-five or have plans to cover your health expenses until that point, I often have clients who incorrectly assume Medicare is their golden ticket to cover all expenses. That is simply not the case.

Retiring Later

Planning for a long life in retirement partly depends on when you retire. While many people end up retiring earlier than they anticipated—due to injuries, layoffs, family crises, and other unforeseen circumstances—continuing to work past age sixty (and even sixty-five) is still a viable option for others and can be an excellent way to help establish financial comfort in retirement.

There are many reasons for this. For one, you obviously still earn a paycheck and the benefits accompanying it. Medical coverage and beefing up your retirement accounts with further savings can be significant by themselves but continuing your income also should keep you from dipping into your retirement funds, further allowing them the opportunity to grow.

Additionally, for many workers, their nine-to-five job is more than just clocking in and out. Having a sense of purpose can keep us active physically, mentally, and socially. That kind of activity

---

https://www.kff.org/report-section/ehbs-2020-section-11-retiree-health-benefits

[5] Fidelity Viewpoints. Fidelity. May 6, 2021. "How to Plan for Rising Health Care Costs." https://www.fidelity.com/viewpoints/personal-finance/plan-for-rising-health-care-costs

and level of engagement may also help stave off many of the health problems that plague retirees. Avoiding a sedentary life is one of the advantages of staying plugged into the workforce, if possible.

Occasionally, I have the experience of attempting to help someone who retired a little early and ran into financial trouble. A lot of times, people finally seek out professional retirement planning help after something catastrophic happens. In almost every case, the client had reached some magical dollar number in their retirement portfolio (the most common being $1 million) and assumed they had made it. I'm not sure what it is about that $1 million figure that causes people to think they have conquered all their financial challenges. Maybe it's that flipping from the six figures to the seven figures. It is a huge accomplishment, that is for sure, but the reality is unless it comes with some sound income and tax planning, you can run into trouble.

New potential clients Ben and Amy were able to amass $1 million in Ben's 401(k) by the time he was sixty. At age fifty-nine and a half, Ben knew he was eligible to start taking withdrawals penalty-free out of that 401(k), and he was itching to pull the trigger on retirement. He felt that $1 million was going to be more than enough for what he and Amy needed, plus he'd be starting his Social Security in six years and that would take over a huge portion of what they would need to live on. Ben felt that was all the income planning they needed.

So, they both retired at the same time, at Ben's age of sixty. They enjoyed traveling and spending time with their grandkids in a different state. The market was good to them and the gains they continued to have on the 401(k) covered their lifestyle completely. Ben started his Social Security at his full retirement age of sixty-six, and Amy did also. They discovered, however, that the combined Social Security was only going to cover about 40 percent of what they would need for their monthly lifestyle. They continued to take withdrawals, although lower, out of Ben's 401(k). It was the summer of 2000.

By the summer of 2001, Ben's 401(k) value had dropped 30 percent from where it was a year earlier, including his withdrawals. Ben and Amy had been through market declines like this before and felt confident things would get back to normal soon. Then September 11, 2001 came. Initially, Ben's account held on. They felt they had been through the worst and would start to see the market rebound. After all, they knew the worst thing they could do now would be to get out of the market and lock in their losses. Unfortunately, by the summer of 2002, Ben's 401(k) had dropped 65 percent from where it had been just two years earlier, including withdrawals: from $1 million down to $351,000. Ben called his 401(k) 1-800 number and liquidated all his positions to cash in an attempt to protect what was left.

I met Ben and Amy in the fall of 2002. They were referred to me by current clients. I am not a miracle worker. There is a limit to what I can repair. It was evident to me that there were challenges they did not understand beyond the losses in the stock market. Like the fact that they would be losing one of their two Social Security payments when the first spouse died, or that it was probable that what they needed to withdraw out of their portfolio would increase, not decrease, because of inflation.

The sad thing about that case is that it did not have to happen. Retiring early was not really the problem! I want my clients to retire early if that is their passion. We had many clients who had similar lifestyle needs and similar assets to Ben and Amy in early 2000 and weathered the storm well, and the next storm that came in 2008. Several of them had retired early, years before they started their Social Security. But they all had retirement income and tax plans.

Health Care

Take a second to reflect on your health care plan. Although working up to or even past age sixty-five would allow you to avoid a coverage gap between your working years and Medicare, that may not be an option for you. Even if it is, when you retire, you will need to make some decisions about what kind of insurance coverage you may need to supplement your Medicare. Are there any medical needs you have that may require coverage in addition to Medicare? Did your parents or grandparents have any inherited medical conditions you might consider using a special savings plan to cover?

These are all questions that are important to review with your financial professional so you can be sure you have enough money put aside for health care.

Long-Term Care

Longevity means the need for long-term care is statistically more likely to happen. If you intend to pass on a legacy, planning for long-term care is paramount, since most estimates project nearly 70 percent of Americans will need some type of it.[6] However, this may be one of the biggest, most stressful pieces of longevity planning I encounter in my work. For one thing, who wants to talk about the point in their lives when they may feel the most limited? Who wants to dwell on what will happen if they no longer can toilet, bathe, dress, or feed themselves?

I get it; this is a less-than-fun part of planning. But a little bit of preparation now can go a long way!

When it comes to your longevity, just like with your goals, one of the important things to do is sit and dream. It may not be the fun, road-trip-to-the-Grand-Canyon kind of dreaming, but you can spend time envisioning how you want your twilight years to look.

For instance, if it is important for you to live in your home for as long as possible, who will provide for the day-to-day fixes and to-dos of housework if you become ill? Will you set aside money for a service, or do you have relatives or friends nearby whom you

[6] LongTermCare.gov. February 18, 2020. "How Much Care Will You Need?" https://acl.gov/ltc/basic-needs/how-much-care-will-you-need

could comfortably allow to help you? Do you prefer in-home care over a nursing home or assisted living? This could be a good time to discuss the possibility of moving into a retirement community versus staying where you are or whether it's worth moving to another state and leaving relatives behind.

These are all important factors to discuss with your spouse and children, as *now* is the right time to address questions and concerns. For instance, is aging in place more important to one spouse than the other? Are the friends or relatives who live nearby emotionally, physically, and financially capable of helping you for a time if you face an illness?

Many families I meet with find these conversations very uncomfortable, particularly when children discuss nursing home care with their parents. A knee-jerk reaction for many is to promise they will care for their aging parents. This is noble and well-intentioned, but there needs to be an element of realism here. Does "help" from an adult child mean they stop by and help you with laundry, cooking, home maintenance, and bills? Or does it mean they move you into their spare room when you have hip surgery? Are they prepared to help you use the restroom and bathe if that becomes difficult for you to do on your own?

I don't mean to discourage families from caring for their own; this can be a profoundly admirable relationship when it works out. However, I've seen families put off planning for late-in-life care based on a tenuous promise that the adult children would care for their parents, only to watch as the support system crumbles. Sometimes this is because the assumed caregiver hasn't given serious thought to the preparation they would need, both in a formal sense and regarding their personal physical, emotional, and financial commitments. This is often also because we can't see the future: Alzheimer's disease and other maladies of old age can exact a heavy toll. When a loved one reaches the point where he or she is at risk of wandering away or needs help with two or more activities of daily living, it can be more than one person or family can realistically handle.

If you know what you want, communicate with your family about both the best-case and worst-case scenarios. Then, hope for the best, and plan for the worst.

Realistic Cost of Care

Wrapped up in your planning should be a consideration for the cost of long-term care. One study estimates that by 2030, the nation's long-term care costs could reach $2.5 trillion as roughly 24 million Americans require some type of long-term care.[7] The potential costs for such care and treatment can be underestimated, especially by those who have maintained robust health and find it difficult to envision future declines to their condition.

Another piece of planning for long-term care costs is anticipating inflation. It's common knowledge that prices have been and keep rising, which can lower your purchasing power on everything from food to medical care. Long-term care is a big piece of the inflation-disparity pie.

While local costs vary from state to state, here's the national median for various forms of long-term care (plus projections that account for a 3 percent annual inflation, so you can see what I am referencing):[8]

[7] Tara O'Neill Hayes, Sara Kurtovic. Americanactionforum.org. February 18, 2020. "The Ballooning Costs of Long-Term Care." https://www.americanactionforum.org/research/the-ballooning-costs-of-long-term-care

[8] Genworth Financial. January 2022. "Cost of Care Survey 2021." https://www.genworth.com/aging-and-you/finances/cost-of-care.html

Long-Term Care Costs: Inflation				
	Home Health Care, Homemaker Services	Adult Day Care	Assisted Living	Nursing Home (semi-private room)
Annual 2021	$59,488	$20,280	$54,000	$94,900
Annual 2031	$79,947	$27,255	$72,571	$127,538
Annual 2041	$107,442	$36,628	$97,530	$171,400
Annual 2051	$144,393	$49,225	$131,072	$230,347

Fund Your Long-Term Care

One critical mistake I see are those who haven't planned for long-term care because they assume the government will provide everything. But that's a big misconception. The government has two health insurance programs: Medicare and Medicaid. These can greatly assist you in your health care needs in retirement but usually don't provide enough coverage to cover all your health care costs in retirement. My firm isn't a government outpost, so we don't get to make decisions when it comes to forming policy and specifics about either one of these programs. I'm going to give an overview of both, but if you want to dive into the details of these programs, you can visit www.Medicare.gov and www.Medicaid.gov.

Medicare

Medicare covers those aged sixty-five and older and those who are disabled. Medicare's coverage of any nursing-home-related health issues is limited. It might cover your nursing home stay if it is not a "custodial" stay, and it isn't long-term. For example, if you break a bone or suffer a stroke, stay in a nursing home for rehabilitative care, and then return home, Medicare may cover you. But, if you have developed dementia or are looking to move to a nursing facility because you can no longer bathe, dress, toilet, feed yourself, or take care of your hygiene, etc., then Medicare is not going to pay for your nursing home costs.[9]

You can enroll in Medicare anytime during the three months before and three months after your sixty-fifth birthday. Miss your enrollment deadline, and you could risk paying increased premiums for the rest of your life.[10] On top of prompt enrollment, there are a few other things to think about when it comes to Medicare, not least among them being the need to understand the different "parts," what they do, and what they don't cover.

Part A

Medicare Part A is what you might think of as "classic" Medicare. Hospital care, some types of home health care, and major medical care fall under this. While most enrollees pay nothing for this service (as they likely paid into the system for at least ten years), you may end up paying, either based on work history or delayed signup. In 2022, the highest premium is $499 per month, and a hospital stay does have a deductible, $1,556.[11] And, if you have a

---

[9] Medicare.gov. "What Part A covers." https://www.medicare.gov/what-medicare-covers/part-a/what-part-a-covers.html

[10] Medicare.gov. "When can I sign up for Medicare?" https://www.medicare.gov/basics/get-started-with-medicare/sign-up/when-can-i-sign-up-for-medicare

[11] Medicare. "Medicare 2022 Costs at a Glance." https://www.medicare.gov/your-medicare-costs/medicare-costs-at-a-glance

hospital stay that surpasses sixty days, you could be looking at additional costs; keep in mind, Medicare doesn't pay for long-term care and services.

Part B

Medicare Part B is an essential piece of wrap-around coverage for Medicare Part A. It helps pay for doctor visits and outpatient services. This also comes with a price tag: Although the Part B deductible is only $233 in 2022, you will still pay 20 percent of all costs after that, with no limit on out-of-pocket expenses.[12]

Part C

Medicare Part C, more commonly known as Medicare Advantage plans, are an alternative to a combination of Parts A, B, and sometimes D. Administered through private insurance companies, these have a variety of costs and restrictions, and they are subject to the specific policies and rules of the issuing carrier.

Part D

Medicare Part D is also through a private insurer and is supplemental to Parts A and B, as its primary purpose is to cover prescription drugs. Like any private insurance plan, Part D has its quirks and rules that vary from insurer to insurer.

The Donut Hole

Even with a "Part D" in place, you may still have a coverage gap between what your Part D private drug insurance pays for your prescription and what basic Medicare pays. In 2022, the coverage gap is $4,430, meaning, after you meet your private prescription insurance limit, you will spend no more than 25 percent of your

---

[12] Ibid.

drug costs out-of-pocket before Medicare will kick in to pay for more prescription drugs.[13]

Medicare Supplements

Medicare Supplement Insurance, MedSupp, Medigap, or plans labeled Medicare Part F, G, H, I, J . . . Known by a variety of monikers, this is just a fancy way of saying "medical coverage for those over sixty-five that picks up the tab for whatever the federal Medicare program(s) doesn't." Again, costs, limitations, etc., vary by carrier.

Does that sound like a bunch of government alphabet soup to you? It certainly does to me. And, did you read the fine print? Unpredictable costs, varied restrictions, difficult-to-compare benefits, donut holes, and coverage gaps. That's par for the course with health care plans through the course of our adult lives. What gives? I thought Medicare was supposed to be easier, comprehensive, and at no cost!

The truth is there is no stage of life when health care is easy to understand.

The best thing you can do for yourself is to scope out the health care field early, compare costs often, and prepare for out-of-pocket costs well in advance—decades, if possible.

Medicaid

Medicaid is a program the states administer, so funding, protocol, and limitations vary. Compared to Medicare, Medicaid more widely covers nursing home care, but it targets a different demographic: those with low incomes.

If you have more assets than the Medicaid limit in your state and need nursing home care, you will need to use those assets to

---

[13] Medicare. "Costs in the coverage gap."
https://www.medicare.gov/drug-coverage-part-d/costs-for-medicare-drug-coverage/costs-in-the-coverage-gap

pay for your care. You will also have a list of additional state-approved ways to spend some of these assets over the Medicaid limit, such as pre-purchasing burial plots and funeral expenses or paying off debts. After that, your remaining assets fund your nursing home stay until they are gone, at which point Medicaid will jump in.

Some people aren't stymied by this, thinking they will just pass on their financial assets early, gifting them to relatives, friends, and causes so they can qualify for Medicaid when they need it. However, to prevent this exact scenario, Uncle Sam has implemented the look-back period. Currently, if you enroll in Medicaid, you are subject to having the government scrutinize the last five years of your finances for large gifts or expenses that may subject you to penalties, temporarily making you ineligible for Medicaid coverage.

So, if you're planning to preserve your money for future generations and retain control of your financial resources during your lifetime, you'll probably want to prepare for the costs of longevity beyond a "government plan."

Self-Funding

One way to fund a longer life is the old-fashioned way, through self-funding. There are a variety of financial tools you can use, and they all have their pros and cons. If your assets are in low-interest financial vehicles (savings, bonds, CDs), you risk letting inflation erode the value of your dollar. Or, if you are relying on the stock market, you have more growth potential, but you'll also want to consider the possible implications of market volatility. What if your assets take a hit? If you suffer a loss in your retirement portfolio in early or mid-retirement, you might have the option to "tighten your belt," so to speak, and cut back on discretionary spending to allow your portfolio the room to bounce back. But, if you are retired and depend on income from a stock account that just hit a downward stride, what are you going to do?

HSAs

These days, you might also be able to self-fund through a health savings account, or HSA, if you have access to one through a high-deductible health plan (you will not qualify to save in an HSA after enrolling in Medicare). In an HSA, any growth of your tax-deductible contributions will be tax-free, and any distributions paid out for qualified health costs are also tax-free. Long-term care expenses count as health costs, so, if this is an option available to you, it is one way to use the tax advantages to self-fund your longevity. Bear in mind, if you are younger than sixty-five, any money you use for nonqualified expenses will be subject to taxes and penalties, and, if you are older than sixty-five, any HSA money you use for non-medical expenses is subject to income tax.

LTCI

One slightly more nuanced way to pay for longevity, specifically for long-term care, is long-term care insurance, or LTCI. As car insurance protects your assets in case of a car accident and home insurance protects your assets in case something happens to your house, long-term care insurance aims to protect your assets in case you need long-term care in an at-home or nursing home situation.

As with other types of insurance, you will pay a monthly or annual premium in exchange for an insurance company paying for long-term care down the road. Typically, policies cover two to three years of care, which is adequate for an "average" situation: it's estimated 70 percent of Americans will need about three years of long-term care of some kind. However, it's important to consider you might not be "average" when you are preparing for long-term care costs; on average, 20 percent of today's sixty-five-year-olds could need care for longer than five years.[14]

---

[14] LongTermCare.gov. February 18, 2020. "How Much Care Will You Need?" https://acl.gov/ltc/basic-needs/how-much-care-will-you-need

Now, there are a few oft-cited components of LTCI that make it unattractive for some:

- Expense — LTCI can be expensive. It is generally less expensive the younger you are, but a fifty-five-year-old couple who purchased LTCI in 2022 could expect to pay $2,080 each year for an average three-year coverage policy. And the annual cost only increases from there the older you are.[15]

- Limited options — Let's face it: LTCI may be expensive for consumers, but it can also be expensive for companies that offer it. With fewer companies willing to take on that expense, this narrows the market, meaning opportunities to price shop for policies with different options or custom benefits are limited.

- If you know you need it, you might not be able to get it — Insurance companies offering LTCI are taking on a risk that you may need LTCI. That risk is the foundation of the product—you may or may not need it. If you know you will need it because you have a dementia diagnosis or another illness for which you will need long-term care, you will likely not qualify for LTCI coverage.

- Use it or lose it — If you have LTCI and are in the minority of Americans who die having never needed long-term care, all the money you paid into your LTCI policy is gone.

- Possibly fluctuating rates — Your rate is not locked in on LTCI. Companies maintain the ability to raise or lower your premium amounts. This means some seniors face an ultimatum: Keep funding a policy at what might be a less affordable rate *or* lose coverage and let go of all the money they paid in so far.

---

[15] American Association for Long-Term Care Insurance. 2022. "Long-Term Care Insurance Facts-Data-Statistics-2022 Reports." https://www.aaltci.org/long-term-care-insurance/learning-center/ltcfacts-2022.php#2022costs

After that, you might be thinking, "How can people possibly be interested in LTCI?" But let me repeat myself—as many as 70 percent of Americans will need long-term care. And, although only one in ten Americans have purchased LTCI, keep in mind the high cost of nursing home care. Can you afford $7,000 a month to put into nursing home care and still have enough left over to protect your legacy? This is a very real concern considering one set of statistics reported a two-in-three chance that a senior citizen will become physically or cognitively impaired in their lifetime.[16] So, not to sound like a broken record, but it is vitally important to have a plan in place to deal with longevity and long-term care if you intend to leave a financial legacy.

I believe the expense you could have if you became incapacitated is the most misunderstood thing in finance today. Many misguided thoughts and ideas come from this realm. Comments I have heard range from, "Well, I will never allow that to happen to me," to, "I'm gonna give all my money to my kids if I get sick so the government doesn't take it."

The reality is that at the beginning of my career in 1992, about one out of three of my clients would probably need some form of long-term care. Today, that number has grown to one out of every two. The typical experience with long-term care lasts three and a half years and costs an average of about $9,000 per month in Illinois, as of this writing.

If you are incapacitated, you don't get to choose if you get long-term care. Someone is going to give it to you. Maybe your thoughts are that a family member will take care of you. Many people are all living longer, healthier lives, sometimes even surviving the cancers and the heart attacks that killed us thirty years ago. But this longevity has created an entirely new medical problem: aging to a point where we become so incapacitated that professional skilled nursing care becomes mandatory. Unless your child is a registered nurse willing to quit his or her full-time

---

[16] payingforseniorcare.com. 2022. "Long-Term Senior Care Statistics." https://www.payingforseniorcare.com/statistics

job to take care of you sixty hours per week, you are going to have to get professional help.

If you are reading this book, that tells me you probably have some money, and that means that the state is not going to pay for your long-term care. You are. There is no way around that. One way or another, you are going to pay for your long-term care if you become incapacitated. The real question is, how are you going to pay for that long-term care?

Who is at greatest financial risk if you become incapacitated? Well, believe it or not, I do not think it is you. If you are married, the person with the greatest financial risk is your spouse. If you become incapacitated, your needs will be taken care of. The real question is, what kind of financial situation is your spouse going to be left in after you burn through a bunch of your nest egg? Is he or she going to be able to maintain anything even remotely close to the lifestyle they had before? On top of dealing with your medical problems, are they going to have to move out of the house because they can't afford it anymore? If you are a single person, your beneficiaries are the ones with the greatest financial risk. If one of your passions was to leave a legacy to them, a mark of a lifetime of hard work and dedication, are you OK with that not happening because you got sick?

Planning for long-term care could be as simple as making sure that you have enough money to be self-insured for the future and still support your lifestyle and legacy today. This is something that our Retirement Blueprint program does even at a very basic level. But I would suggest that you do a little bit beyond that. You could consider buying long-term care insurance, but I find that using life insurance might be a much more powerful consideration. If you buy long-term care insurance, you may or may not get sick. But if you buy life insurance, you are going to use it, undoubtedly. We are all going to die. If that life insurance is structured properly, it should pay a death benefit when you are gone, guaranteed. That death benefit could act as a hedge to protect your nest egg for your spouse and leave a legacy for other beneficiaries.

A few relevant statistics to keep in mind:

- The longer you live, the more likely you are to continue living; the longer you live, the more health care you will likely need to pay for.
- The average cost of a private nursing home room in the United States in 2021 was $9,034 a month.[17] But keep in mind, that is just the nursing home—it doesn't include other medical costs, let alone pleasantries, like entertainment or hobby spending.
- In 2021, Fidelity calculated that a healthy couple retiring at age sixty-five could expect to pay around $300,000 over the course of retirement to cover health and medical expenses.
- The average man will need $143,00, and the average woman needs about 10 percent more, or $157,000, because of women's longer life expectancies.[18]

I know. Whoa, there, Ed, I was hoping to have a realistic idea of health costs, not be driven over by a cement mixer!

The good news is, while we don't know these exact costs in advance, we know there *will* be costs. And you won't have to pay your total Medicare lifetime premiums in one day as a lump sum. Now that you have a good idea of health care costs in retirement, you can *plan* for them! That's the real point, here: Planning in advance can keep you from feeling nickel-and-dimed to your wits' end. Instead, having a sizeable portion of your assets earmarked for health care can allow you the freedom to choose health care

---

[17] Genworth Financial. January 31, 2022. "Genworth 2020 Cost of Care Survey." https://www.genworth.com/aging-and-you/finances/cost-of-care.html

[18] Elizabeth O'Brien. Money. May 10, 2021. "Health Care Now Costs Couples $300,000 in Retirement, According to Fidelity's Latest Estimate." https://money.com/health-care-costs-retirement-fidelity-2021-study/. The $300,000 estimate assumes an opposite-gender couple, where the man lives until age 87 and the woman until age 89.

networks, coverage options, and long-term care possibilities you like and that you think offer you the best in life.

Product Riders

LTCI and self-funding are not the only ways to plan for the expenses of longevity. Some companies are getting creative with their products, particularly insurance companies. One way they are retooling to meet people's needs is through optional product riders on annuities and life insurance. Elsewhere in this book, I talk about annuity basics, but here's a brief overview: Annuities are insurance contracts. You pay the insurance company a premium, either as a lump sum or as a series of payments over a set amount of time, in exchange for guaranteed income payments. One of the advantages of an annuity is it has access to riders, which allow you to tweak your contract for a fee, usually about 1 percent of the contract value annually. One annuity rider some companies offer is a long-term care rider. If you have an annuity with a long-term care rider and are not in need of long-term care, your contract behaves as any annuity contract would—nothing changes. Generally speaking, if you reach a point when you can't perform multiple functions of daily life on your own, you notify the insurance company, and a representative will turn on those provisions of your contract.

Like LTCI, different companies and products offer different options. Some annuity long-term care riders offer coverage of two years in a nursing home situation. Others cap expenses at two times the original annuity's value. It greatly depends. Some people prefer this option because there isn't a "use-it-or-lose-it" piece; if you die without ever having needed long-term care, you still will have had the income benefit from the base contract. Still, as with any annuities or insurance contracts, there are the usual restrictions and limitations. Withdrawing money from the contract will affect future income payments, early distributions can result in a penalty, income taxes may apply, and, because the insurance company's solvency is what guarantees your payments, it's important to do your research about the insurance company you are considering purchasing a contract from.

Understandably, a discussion on long-term care is bound to feel at least a little tedious. Yet, this is a critical piece of planning for income in retirement, particularly if you want to leave a legacy.

A normal part of our process is to explain financial threats to our clients, and this is a big one. I had a couple as clients to whom I explained the financial threat of one of them becoming incapacitated in detail when we first met in 2005. We will call them Mike and Pam for the sake of this story. Mike and Pam hired us to do a Retirement Blueprint. They were both sixty-five at the time and had $700,000 saved up in retirement accounts. They decided to take our suggestions for income planning and growth planning and followed through with several of our tax planning suggestions.

However, they decided not to take our suggestions when it came to long-term care planning. They were both in good health and were physically very fit, but they had the mentality of "that will never happen to me—or at least not for another fifteen years or so." I explained to them that although we had a great battle plan in place to protect their income, be proactive on taxes, and still take advantage of the markets, if either of them needed long-term care, it would put the surviving spouse in financial jeopardy. It would be the financial equivalent of Hurricane Katrina. Regardless, they decided to put off thinking about that until a later date.

Several years went by of annual reviews where I brought up the subject. Every time, it was put off. I kind of got the sense they were getting a little irritated by me continuing to bring it up every review meeting.

Then one year, we reached out for our normal annual review, and Pam told us that they could not make it. Mike had a stroke. He had to learn how to walk and talk again from scratch and had the use of his left arm but not the right (of course he was right-handed). The use of the right arm never returned. After fighting to learn how to walk and talk again, Mike had a second stroke about twelve months after the first.

He was only seventy-one years old.

After the second stroke, Mike never walked again. He was able to stabilize, but he had to have round-the-clock long-term care. The nightmare scenario had become a reality. At first, Pam was able to care for him herself. But soon, Mike's needs surpassed what Pam could do for him, and a registered nurse had to come to the house. This expense was not covered by Medicare or any of their supplemental insurance. This was long-term care. The bills escalated quickly and the withdrawals out of the nest egg got larger and larger. Mike eventually had to move into a long-term care facility. He fought a long, hard fight but passed away at seventy-six, six years after all of this began.

Although when I first met them at age sixty-five, the $700,000 nest egg was plenty of money for their lifestyle needs, the unprotected and unplanned for threat of long-term care expenses obliterated that dream. Approximately $350,000 of the nest egg went toward Mike's care. Pam was left with significantly reduced funds to live on, and only one out of the two Social Security payments. Pam's lifestyle changed significantly to fit her new financial reality, and it never recovered.

Spousal Planning

Here's one thing to keep in mind no matter how you plan to save: Many of us will be planning for more than ourselves. Look back at all the stats on health events and the likelihood of long life and long-term care. If they hold true for a single individual, then the likelihood of having a costly health or long-term care event is even higher for a married couple. You'll be planning for not just one life, but two. So, when it comes to long-term care insurance, annuities, self-funding, or whatever strategy you are looking at using, be sure you are funding longevity for the both of you.

The worst part about Mike and Pam's story is that it didn't have to be that way. I believe the planning would have protected them. The problem is that a lot of people don't want to think about long-term care because it is such a morbid concept, and then, in many cases, they don't want to make the sacrifice needed (spending the money) to hedge against this threat.

CHAPTER 2

Taxes

Where to begin with taxes? Perhaps by acknowledging we all bear responsibility for the resources we share. Roads, bridges, schools . . . It is the patriotic duty of every American to pay their fair share of taxes. Many would agree with me. However, while they don't mind paying their fair share, they're not interested in paying one cent more than that!

Now, just talking taxes probably takes your mind to April—tax season. You are probably thinking about all the forms you collect and how you file. Perhaps you are thinking about your certified public accountant or another qualified tax professional and saying to yourself, "I've already got taxes taken care of, thanks!"

However, what I see when people come into my office is that their relationship with their tax professional is purely a January through April relationship. That means they may have a tax professional, but not a tax *planner*.

What I mean is tax planning extends beyond filing taxes. In April, we are required to settle our accounts with the IRS to make sure we have paid up on our bill or to even the score if we have overpaid. But real tax planning is about making each financial move in a way that allows you to keep the most money in your pocket and out of Uncle Sam's.

Now, as a caveat, I want to emphasize I am neither a CPA nor a tax planner, but I see the way taxes affect my clients, and I have plenty of experience helping clients implement tax-efficient

25

strategies in their retirement plans in conjunction with their tax professionals.

I have had a strategic partnership with a certified public accountant (CPA) since I began my career in 1992. As I mentioned earlier, my Uncle Marty was a CPA and worked closely with my father, Ed Sr., the estate planning attorney. Dad did the legal work, Uncle Marty did the tax preparation and tax planning (especially for clients that had small businesses), and I was brought in to execute financial products. Really, at the beginning of my career, I was a financial order-taker for whatever my dad and Uncle Marty told me.

This gave me a very sound foundation for understanding the importance of having tax planning integrated into the total retirement picture. I also discovered that this was one of the most underserved areas in my profession. Most financial advisors focus all their energies on the creation of wealth but very little on trying to keep that wealth!

As my career progressed, I met several CPAs which catalyzed the opening of my own private firm, Downey Financial Group, in 2002. Over the first twenty years, Downey Financial Group produced thousands and thousands of tax returns prepared by staff CPAs. We completed tax returns for our financial clients and the general public. In fact, preparing taxes for the public was one of the key strategies we had to meet new potential retirement planning clients.

The tax preparation service and the relationship with the CPAs led to a very detailed understanding of our clients' 1040 tax returns. I am not a CPA, but because of my experience, I am able to talk intelligently to any one of them in regard to almost every line of the 1040. This, combined with my financial planning knowledge, makes Downey Financial Group extremely powerful when it comes to tax planning for our clients.

Although we no longer offer tax preparation to the general public, the service of making sure our clients' tax return is completed perfectly by a CPA is a core principle of our firm.

It is especially important to me to help my clients develop tax-efficient strategies in their retirement plans because each dollar they can keep in their pockets is a dollar we can put to work.

You have probably read this somewhere before, but just in case you haven't: "It's not about how much you make, it's about how much you get to keep after taxes."

The Fed

Now, in the United States, taxes can be a rather uncertain proposition. Depending on who is in the White House and which party controls Congress, we might be tempted to assume tax rates could either decline or increase in the next four to eight years accordingly. However, there is one (large!) factor we, as a nation, must confront: the national debt.

Currently, according to USDebtClock.org, we are over $29,000,000,000,000 in debt and climbing. That's $29 *trillion* with a "T." With just $1 trillion, you could park it in the bank at a zero percent interest rate and spend more than $54 million every day for fifty years without hitting a zero balance.

Even if Congress got a handle and stopped that debt from its daily compound, divided by each taxpayer, we each would owe about $214,000. So, will that be check, cash, or Venmo?

My point here isn't to give you anxiety. I'm just cautioning you that even with the rosiest of outlooks on our personal income tax rates, none of us should count on low tax rates for the long term. Instead, you and your network of professionals (tax, legal, and financial) should constantly be looking for ways to take advantage of tax-saving opportunities as they come. After all, the best "luck" is when proper planning meets opportunity.

So, how can we get started?

Know Your Limits

One of the foundational pieces of tax planning is knowing what tax bracket you are in, based on your income after subtracting pre-tax or untaxed assets. Your income taxes are based on your taxable income.

One reason to know your taxable income and your income tax rate is so you can see how far away you are from the next lower or higher tax bracket. This is particularly important when it comes to decisions such as gifting and Roth IRA rollovers.

For instance, based on the 2022 tax table, Mallory and Ralph's taxable income is just over $345,000, putting them in the 32 percent tax bracket and about $4,900 above the upper end of the 24 percent tax bracket. They have already maxed out their retirement funds' tax-exempt contributions for the year. Their daughter, Gloria, is a sophomore in college. This couple could shave a considerable amount off their tax bill if they use the $4,900 to help Gloria out with groceries and school—something they were likely to do, anyway, but now can deliberately be put to work for them in their overall financial strategy.

Now, I use Mallory and Ralph only as an example—your circumstances are probably different—but I think this nicely illustrates the way planning ahead for taxes can save you money.

Assuming a Lower Tax Rate

Many people anticipate being in a lower tax bracket in retirement. It makes sense: You won't be contributing to retirement funds; you'll be drawing from them. And you won't have all those work expenses—work clothes, transportation, lunch meetings, etc.

Yet, do you really plan on changing your lifestyle after retirement? Do you plan to cut down on the number of times you eat out, scale back vacations, and skimp on travel?

What I see in my office is many couples spend more in the first few years, or maybe the first decade, of retirement. Sure, that may taper off later on, but usually only just in time for them to be hit with greater health and long-term care expenses. Do you see where this is going? Many people plan as though their taxable income will be lower in retirement and are surprised when the tax bills come in and look more or less the same as they used to. It's better to plan for the worst and hope for the best, wouldn't you agree?

401(k)/IRA

One sometimes-unexpected piece of tax planning in retirement concerns your 401(k) or IRA. Most of us have one of these accounts or an equivalent. Throughout our working lives, we pay in, dutifully socking away a portion of our earnings in these tax-deferred accounts. There's the rub: tax-deferred. Not tax-free. Very rarely is anything free of taxation when you get down to it. Using 401(k)s and IRAs in retirement is no different. The taxes the government deferred when you were in your working years are now coming due, and you will pay taxes on that income at whatever your current tax rate is.

Just to ensure Uncle Sam gets his due, the government also has a required minimum distribution, or RMD, rule. Beginning at age seventy-two, you are required to withdraw a certain minimum amount every year from your 401(k) or IRA, or else you will face a 50 percent tax penalty on any RMD monies you should have withdrawn but didn't—and that's on top of income tax.

Of course, there is also the Roth account. You can think of the difference between a Roth and a traditional retirement account as the difference between taxing the seed and taxing the harvest. Because Roths are funded with post-tax dollars, there aren't tax penalties for early withdrawals of the principal nor are there taxes on the growth after you reach age fifty-nine-and-one-half. Perhaps best of all, there are no RMDs. Of course, you must own a Roth account for a minimum of five years before you are able to take advantage of all its features.

This is one more area where it pays to be aware of your tax bracket. Some people may find it advantageous to "convert" their traditional retirement account funds to Roth account funds in a year during which they are in a lower tax bracket. Others may opt to put any excess RMDs from their traditional retirement accounts into other products, like stocks or insurance.

Does that make your head spin? Understandable. That's why it's so important to work with a financial professional and tax planner who can help you execute these sorts of tax-efficient strategies and help you understand what you are doing and why.

So, why don't people put a lot of effort into tax planning? For that matter, why don't CPAs do a lot of tax planning? Many CPAs (maybe even yours if you have one) do a good job at making sure your tax return is completed correctly and filed on time. A really good CPA will also make sure you are not missing any tax deductions or tax breaks offered by the IRS for that tax year. But that is not tax planning. Planning is something you do for the future. What I just described is tax reporting. It is what has happened in the past. Most CPAs are good tax reporters but terrible tax planners.

I think the reason for this is CPAs are not paid to be tax planners (usually). They are paid to be tax reporters. When you seek out a CPA, it is typically because you want your tax return done for the previous year. Or you got a scary letter from the IRS about a past tax year, and you are freaking out and want professional help.

I have never heard of someone paying a CPA to do planning on a hypothetical future individual 1040 tax return. However, hypothetical future tax planning is exactly what a good financial advisor does.

I had a client, we'll call him Chuck, who really wanted to retire when he was sixty-five. I met him when he was sixty. Chuck was a very involved planning client. He had a strong relationship with his CPA; she was his sister. When I met him, he had already calculated what his and his wife's probable lifestyle expenses were going to be (including fun!) by the time they were sixty-five.

He also calculated a 20 percent buffer for income taxes. So that meant based on his calculations they would only net out about 80 percent of their gross Social Security and withdrawals from their retirement investments. Chuck hired us to do a Retirement Blueprint, and through some good withdrawal structure, we were able to get him at a 0 percent income tax rate for the first few years of his retirement, and then only a 5 percent rate after he turned age seventy. This meant Chuck had a ton of extra cash flow, and that resulted in Chuck retiring early at age sixty-one! Chuck was always an avid golfer and got his handicap down from twenty-three to nine by the time he was age sixty-three.

CHAPTER 3

Market Volatility

U p and down. Roller coaster. Merry-go-round. Bulls and bears. Peak-to-trough.

Sound familiar? This is the language we use to talk about the stock market. With volatility and spikes, even our language is jarring, bracing, and vivid.

Still, financial strategies tend to revolve around market-based products, for good reasons. For one thing, there is no other financial class that packs the same potential for growth, pound for pound, as stock-based products. Because of growth potential, inflation protection, and new opportunities, it may be unwise to avoid the market entirely.

However, along with the potential for growth is the potential for loss. Many of the people I see in my office come in still feeling a bit burned from the market drama of 2000 to 2010. That was a rough stretch, and many of us are once-bitten-twice-shy investors, right?

So how do we balance these factors? How do we try to satisfy both the need for protection and the need for growth?

For one thing, it is important to recognize the value of diversity. Now, I'm not just talking about the diversity of assets among different kinds of stocks, or even different kinds of stocks and bonds. That's only one kind of diversity; while important, both stocks and bonds, though different, are both still market-based products. Most market-based products, even within a diverse portfolio, tend to rise or lower as a whole, just like an incoming tide. Therefore, a portfolio diverse in only market-sourced products won't automatically protect your assets during times when the market declines.

In addition to the sort of "horizontal diversity" you have by purchasing a variety of stocks and bonds from different companies, I also suggest you think about "vertical diversity," or diversity among asset classes. This means having different product types, including securities products, bank products, and insurance products—with varying levels of growth potential, liquidity, and protection—all in accordance with your unique situation, goals, and needs.

There are two things I can tell you absolutely, positively about the stock and bond markets. They are going to go up and they are going to go down. The problem is, we don't know just how much or when. If you meet someone who thinks they do know how much and/or when, run as fast as you can in the other direction. Only God knows that. I do not believe market timing works.

I do, however, believe that a good long-term growth stock market investment philosophy will produce results. The problem here is that there are multiple good philosophies. There are too many to get into in this book. I have seen several that work great. In most cases, I find having a mixture of philosophies is best, since some work better than others in various market conditions. Before you invest in anything, make sure you have a basic understanding of what you are getting into.

You would not get behind the wheel of a car if you did not know at least the basics of how a car works, such as how to put it into drive or the difference between the gas pedal and the brake. That does not mean you can recite the timing differential of the V-8 engine. You don't have to know that. You just need to know the basics. Your investments should be no different. If they are too complicated for you to understand, you probably should not invest in them.

Many people focus all their financial planning energy on making as much money as possible in the stock market. Don't get me wrong—there is nothing wrong with making a lot of money. I am all for that! But just making a lot of money may not get you to your goals. You can make a lot of money in the markets, get exceptional rates of return, and still run out of money in retirement.

The real problem here is that just saving as much as you can from work and then earning as much as you can on your investments is not goal-orientated. There is no "finish line" with that type of approach. Who knows if you are on track with that nest egg you're working so hard to build? Maybe you need to adjust your savings somehow to catch up, or maybe you have already overfunded what you need and could retire sooner or have a higher lifestyle income.

We spend the bulk of our lives in the working phase (we also call this the asset accumulation phase) where it is all about accumulating. Saving as much as we can. Making as much as we can at work. Raising kids if we have kids. Paying off mortgages if we have mortgages. And then making more money at work again. Repeat.

However, when we get to the next phase, the retirement phase (we also call it the income phase) what we want our money to do changes 180 degrees. It's not about having the highest income in the land. It's about having just enough income to pay for the lifestyle that we desire. At this phase, your financial needs become very goal-orientated. There is a set income number that you are trying to produce every month. I believe this is a quantifiable number, meaning every number can be itemized into an actual typical monthly cost. Once you have that number, you now have the key to unlock your retirement puzzle. You will have the ability to forecast your needs with inflation, with different expenses coming on and falling off as you get older. You now have a rolling financial target you are trying to hit for the rest of your life. You have a goal!

The Color of Money

When you're looking at the overall diversity of your portfolio, part of the equation is knowing which products fit in what category: what has liquidity, what has protection, and what has growth potential.

Before we dive in, keep in mind these aren't absolutes. You might think of liquidity, growth, and protection as primary colors. While some products will look pretty much yellow, red, or blue, others will have a mix of characteristics, making them more green, orange, or purple.

Growth

I like to think of the growth category as red. It's powerful, it's somewhat volatile, and it's also the category where we have the greatest opportunities for growth and loss. Often, products in the growth category will have a good deal of liquidity but very little protection. These are our market-based products and strategies, and we think of them mostly in shades of red and orange, to designate their growth and liquidity. This is a good place to be when you're young—think fast cars and flashy leather jackets—but its allure often wanes as you move closer to retirement. Examples of "red" products include:

- Stocks
- Equities
- Exchange-traded funds
- Mutual funds
- Corporate bonds
- Real estate investment trusts
- Speculations
- Alternative investments

Liquidity

Yellow is my liquid category color. I typically recommend having at least enough yellow money to cover six months' to a year's worth of expenses in case of emergency. Yellow assets don't need a lot of growth potential; they just need to be readily available when we need them. The "yellow" category includes assets like:
- Cash
- Money market accounts

Protection

The color of protection, to me, is blue. Tranquil, peaceful, sure, even if it lacks a certain amount of flash. This is the direction I like to see people generally move toward as they're nearing retirement. The red, flashy look of stock market returns and the risk of possible overnight losses is less attractive as we near retirement and look for more consistency and reliability. While this category doesn't come with a lot of liquidity, the products here are backed by an insurance company, a bank, or a government entity. "Blue" products include things such as:
- Certificates of deposit (backed by banks)
- Government-based bonds (backed by the U.S. government)
- Life insurance (backed by insurance companies)
- Annuities (backed by insurance companies)

What we advocate our clients do is to separate their assets into different piles, or buckets, to fund their retirement income needs. We call this retirement income bucket planning. It is not a new concept by any means. I was first introduced to retirement income bucket planning in the early 1990s as a beginning financial advisor. You should have at least three buckets: One for emergency account needs (I suggest six months of expenses in a savings account), one for income needs, and one more bucket for long-term growth needs.

You may end up having more than three buckets. We have clients who have six or seven buckets: A bucket for their vacation home. A bucket for their grandchildren's college education. Another bucket for a charity. The point here is that your bucket has a specific purpose and goal to drive investment suggestions and decisions—not just to try to make money. At the very least, you'll have three buckets: emergency, income, and growth.

The income bucket is engineered to fund the income needs you will have over your entire retirement. If that is not financially feasible, at least the first ten years of income needs should be funded in the income bucket. This is the bucket that all your regular income withdrawals are going to come from, not any of the other buckets. I believe the investments inside that income bucket should be as conservative or safe as possible. More about that later. All remaining assets could then go into the long-term growth bucket.

401(k)s

I want to take a second to specifically address a product many retirees will be using to build their retirement income: the 401(k) and other retirement accounts. Any of these retirement accounts (IRAs, 401(k)s, 403(b)s, etc.) are basically "tax wrappers." What do I mean by that? Well, depending on your plan provider, a 401(k) could include target-date funds, passively managed products, stocks, bonds, mutual funds, or even variable, fixed, and fixed index annuities, all collected in one place and governed by rules (a.k.a. the "tax wrapper"). These rules govern how much money you can put inside, what ways you can put it in, when you will pay taxes on it, and when you can take the money out. Inside the 401(k), each of the products inside the "tax wrapper" might have its own fees or commissions, in addition to the management fee you pay on the 401(k) itself.

Now, fees can be troublesome. You can't get something for nothing, and fees are how many financial companies and professionals make a living. Yet, it's important to recognize even a fee with a fraction of a percentage point is money out of your pocket—money that represents not just the one-time fee of today but also represents an opportunity cost. A $100,000 IRA that earns 6 percent over a twenty-five-year period without investment fees would earn $430,000. But if just a 0.5 percent fee got factored into that investment, the IRA would be worth $379,000 in twenty-five years, a $50,500 decrease.[19] For someone close to retirement, how much do you think fees may have cost over their lifetime?

Even for those close to retirement, it's important to look at management fees and assess if you think you're getting what you pay for. Over the course of ten years, those costs can add up, and you may have decades ahead of you in which you will need to rely on your assets.

Dollar-Cost Averaging

With 401(k)s and other market-based retirement products, dollar-cost averaging is a concept that can work in your favor when you are investing for the long term. When the market is trending up, if you are consistently paying in money, month over month, great; your investments can grow, and you are adding to your assets. When the market takes a dip, no problem; your dollars buy more shares at a lower price. At some point, we hope the market will rebound, in which case your shares can grow and possibly be more valuable than they were before. This concept is what we call "dollar-cost averaging." While it can't ensure a profit

---

[19] Pam Krueger. Kiplinger.com. January 8, 2021. "How to Spot (and Squash) Nasty Fees That Hide in Your Investments."
https://www.kiplinger.com/retirement/retirement-planning/602043/how-to-spot-and-squash-nasty-fees-that-hide-in-your

or guarantee against losses, it's a time-tested strategy for investing in a volatile market.

However, when you are in retirement, this strategy may work against you. You may have heard of "reverse" dollar-cost averaging. Before, when the market lost ground, you were "bargain-shopping"; your dollars purchased more assets at a reduced price. When you are in retirement, you are no longer the purchaser; you are selling. So, in a down market, you have to sell more assets to make the same amount of money as what you made in a favorable market.

I've had lots of people step into my office to talk to me about this, emphasizing, "my advisor says the market always bounces back, and I have to just hold on for the long term."

There's some basis for this thinking; thus far, the market has always rebounded to higher heights than before. But this is no guarantee, and the prospect of potentially higher returns in five years may not be very helpful in retirement if you are relying on the income from those returns to pay this month's electric bill, for example.

By separating your growth bucket assets from your income and emergency bucket assets, you can invest those growth bucket assets as you see fit.

In many cases, I find new potential clients have let fear start to dictate all their decision-making. They go through market swings and volatility and their gut starts churning. A little voice inside them starts thinking terrible thoughts. What if I run out of money in retirement? What if the stock market has another big crash, and I end up getting sick at the same time or needing a bunch of extra money?

Now, the voice is not wrong. Those are real threats to be concerned with. This is the same voice that tells us not to put our hands on a red-hot stove. Maybe we had to experience the red-hot stove lesson personally, or maybe we learned the fear by watching our brother or sister put their hand on the red-hot stove. But does that mean you never cook on a stove again? Of course not. You're going to use a stove again, but you are going to do it in a safe fashion and not in a reckless high-risk fashion. Plus, if there was a safe alternative to cooking recklessly on the stove, why use the stove in some kind of risky fashion that it was not really intended for?

It is my opinion that once you have your income and emergency buckets funded and secured, the long-term growth bucket can be invested as you see fit. This funding and security buy you the luxury of letting those growth assets deal with the volatility necessary to participate in market volatility and make money long term. Again, the growth bucket is not intended for any of your month-to-month income needs. That all comes out of the income bucket. If all your lifestyle expenses were covered by the income bucket, what kind of a difference would it make regarding how you felt about volatility in the growth bucket? I believe it would give you the support necessary to lower anxiety and fear about what is going on with your investments in the growth bucket. Fear stops running the show. Good decision-making based on your true feelings about risk, opportunity, and reward takes over.

So, what is the purpose of that growth bucket? If it's not being used for month-to-month expenses, what is it supposed to do? The main purpose of the growth bucket is to fund the additional income bucket needs as necessary. I attempt to fund our clients' income bucket with as much money is needed for all income needs for their entire retirement and try to choose products and investments that have the capability of increasing that income to deal with inflation. But what if we have some hyperinflation—like a Jimmy Carter-type inflation experience? It may be necessary for some of that growth bucket money to be poured into the income bucket to increase lifestyle income. That is the main purpose of the growth bucket.

The second purpose of the growth bucket is to be there for those big-ticket irregular expenses: buying a new car, replacing the roof, lending money to your kid (for the thirteenth time), etc.

Beyond that, the growth bucket is the dream machine. As my clients have had successes with their growth bucket assets, profits are taken to go on their dream vacations, buy second homes, fund grandchildren's college, etc.

Is There a "Perfect" Product?

To bring us back around to the discussion of protection, growth, and liquidity, the ideal product would be a "ten" in all three categories, right? Completely guaranteed, doubling in size every few years, and accessible whenever you want. Does such a product exist? Absolutely not.

There is no perfect product, investment, plan, or idea. There is only your plan and solutions, and those are unique and custom to your situation. In many cases with new clients, I discover that they have bought into some investment strategy or product thinking it was a "sure thing" that would solve all their retirement problems. I do not believe such a thing exists. Mom and Dad were right: if it sounds too good to be true, it probably is.

Instead of running in circles looking for that perfect product, the silver bullet, the unicorn of financial strategies, it's more important to circle back to the concept of a balanced, asset-diverse portfolio.

This is why your interests may be best served when you work with a trusted financial professional who knows what various financial products can do and how to use them in your personal retirement strategy.

I meet with a couple of different types of investors.

The first type is the Risk Taker. This is someone who's comfortable with significant volatility and is willing to leave their money alone over long periods of time to go through different market cycles—bull and bear. The Risk Taker usually endures big market swings well during the accumulation phase. They don't freak out when the market drops and stick to the quality investments they had before the calamity started. Then they re-evaluate the quality of their investments when things settle down. I find that this works very well for the Risk Taker, especially if they are reinvesting dividends and contributing new money from work. They may be inadvertently dollar-cost averaging and accomplishing the main goal of investing: buy low and sell high. The accumulation phase can be very successful for the Risk Taker, especially if there have been some corrections or even a bear market along the way.

However, this changes dramatically when the Risk Taker gets to the income phase. The insidious evil here is that the Risk Taker has been conditioned that just staying in and playing the waiting game with the markets will solve all problems. Plus, the Risk Taker has been adding their own money into the kitty for years and that has muddied the actual returns they have been receiving. It has given them the impression that the returns in their investments have been much higher than is reality. This sets them up for a disaster if they were counting on similar returns in retirement and then walk into a big down bear market right at the start.

The second type of investor I meet is the Conservative. This is the type of investor who would freak out about any kind of loss with the money they have worked so hard to accumulate. This would also include any money they inherited. I find that the Conservative has usually endured some type of life challenge that caused them to operate under the principle of not losing money at all costs. They would adjust their lifestyle downward if necessary in order to live within their means. Like the Risk Taker, this has very little impact to their financial condition during the working years. Their lifestyle is totally covered by their work income.

Here, we have another dramatic shift when the Conservative gets to retirement. The reality is that the number one concern, by far, for both the Risk Taker and the Conservative is not making or losing money. The number one concern is running out of money. The Risk Taker can run out of money due to market losses combined with the need for income, but the Conservative can also run out of money because of not earning enough long term to keep up with inflation and real-life emergencies.

In many cases, I have clients where one spouse is the Risk Taker and the other the Conservative. Hey, this is normal, right—opposites attract? I would have to agree with that statement in my marriage. But in many cases with my clients, I find this difference has created a rift between a couple when it comes to their money. Sometimes the Risk Taker is a bit more dominant in the decision-making, sometimes it's the Conservative. So, what do we do here?

Well, I think they are both right. The biggest challenge I see with most people making it through retirement comfortably is taking way more risk than they should with their nest egg. Most people I meet will probably be okay as long as they don't lose a bunch of money. On the other hand, if their portfolio in total is not growing competitively, they may end up running out of money anyway. Not to sound like a broken record, but this is where the bucket income plan structure is fantastic. It pleases both the Risk Taker and the Conservative. In my experience, it causes the total portfolio rate of return to increase because their concerns have been reduced. This allows the client to have a more open mind about their long-term growth investments.

At the end of the day, if the Risk Taker wants a more market-based approach to their Retirement Blueprint, that is fine. If the Conservative wants as little risk as possible with their portfolio, that is fine also. As long as the natural desires of the investor do not conflict with the probable success of the retirement income and tax plan, why fight your nature? I see no reason to force yourself to be risky or conservative if it's not necessary "just because." You are going to have to live with this creation and there is no reason you should be unhappy with it. However, if the reality is that your desires are going to significantly reduce the probability of success of your Retirement Blueprint, you must change your ways. I believe having that balance between the income bucket and the growth bucket–and having the income bucket assets as conservative as possible–brings peace to this issue.

CHAPTER 4

Retirement Income

R etirement. For many of us, it's what we've saved for and dreamed of, pinning our hopes to a magical someday. Is that someday full of traveling? Is it filled with grandkids? Gardening? Maybe your fondest dream is simply never having to work again, never having to clock in or be accountable to someone else.

Your ability to do these things all hinges on *income*. Without the money to support these dreams, even a basic level of work-free lifestyle is unsustainable. That's why planning for your income in retirement is so foundational. But where do we begin?

It's easy to feel overwhelmed by this question. Some may feel the urge to amass a large lump sum and then try to put it all in one product—insurance, investments, liquid assets—to provide all the growth, liquidity, and income they need. Instead, I think you need a more balanced approach. After all, retirement planning isn't magic. Like I mention elsewhere, there is no single product that can be all things to all people (or even all things to one person). No approach works unilaterally for everyone. That's why it's important to talk to a financial professional who can help you lay down the basics and take you step-by-step through the process. Not only will you have the assurance you have addressed the areas you need to, but you will also have an ally who can help you break down the process and help keep you from feeling overwhelmed.

Sources of Income

There are three main topics we find people wanting financial help with: income planning, long-term growth planning, and tax planning. Of the three, which is most important? To me, it's income planning, without a doubt. If you run out of money, you don't have to worry about taxes. You won't be paying taxes anymore because you won't have any money. Long-term growth and the stock market won't be a concern either, also because you won't have any money. This would be like building a house and completing the walls and the roof before you gave any thought to the foundation. My guess is your house will fall down. You cannot do any quality tax or long-term growth planning until the income foundation is set strong and battle-ready.

Thinking of all the pieces of your retirement expenses might be intimidating. But, like cleaning out a junk drawer or revisiting that garage remodel, once you have laid everything out, you can begin to sort things into categories.

Once you have a good overall picture of where your expenses will lie, you can start stacking up the resources to cover them.

Social Security

Social Security is a guaranteed, inflation-protected federal insurance program playing a significant part in most of our retirement plans. From delaying until you've reached full retirement age or beyond to examining spousal benefits, as I discuss elsewhere in this book, there is plenty you can do to try to make the most of this monthly benefit. As with all your retirement income sources, it's important to consider how to make this resource stretch to provide the most bang and buck for your situation.

Pension

Another generally reliable source of retirement income for you might be a pension, if you are one of the lucky people who still has one.

If you don't have a pension, go ahead and skim on to the next section. If you do have a pension, keep on reading.

Because your pension can be such a central piece of your retirement income plan, you will want to put some thought into answering basic questions about it.

How well is your pension funded? Since the heyday of the pension plan, companies and governments have neglected to fund their pension obligations, causing a persistent problem with this otherwise reliable asset. However, research conducted by the Pew Charitable Trusts showed a collective increase in assets exceeding half a trillion dollars in state retirement plans fueled by strong market investment returns in fiscal 2021. Pew's estimates that state retirement systems rose to 80 percent funding for the first time in 2008.[20]

Consider the factors at play, though. Pensions had been underfunded and gained a boost from strong market performance in 2021. What happens to the solvency of those pension funds if the market declines?

It can be worthwhile to keep tabs on your pension's health and know what your options are for withdrawing your pension. If you have already retired and made those decisions, this may be a foregone conclusion. If not, it pays to know what you can expect and what decisions you can make, such as taking spousal options to cover your husband or wife if he or she outlives you.

Also, some companies are incentivizing lump-sum payouts of pensions to reduce the companies' payment liabilities. If that's

---

[20] pewtrusts.org. September 14, 2021. "The State Pension Funding Gap: Plans Have Stabilized in Wake of Pandemic."
https://www.pewtrusts.org/en/research-and-analysis/issue-briefs/2021/09/the-state-pension-funding-gap-plans-have-stabilized-in-wake-of-pandemic

the case with your employer, talk to your financial professional to see if it might be prudent to do something like that or if it might be better to stick with lifetime payments or other options.

Your 401(k) and IRA

One "modern way" to save for retirement is in a 401(k) or IRA (or their nonprofit or governmental equivalents). These tax-advantaged accounts are, in my opinion, a poor substitute for pensions, but one of the biggest disservices we do to ourselves is to not take full advantage of them in the first place. According to one article, only 41 percent of Americans invest in a 401(k), though 68 percent of employed Americans have access to a 401(k) benefit option.[21]

Also, if you have changed jobs over the years, do the work of tracking down any benefits from your past employers. You might have an IRA here or a 401(k) there; keep track of those so you can pull them together and look at those assets when you're ready to look at establishing sources of retirement income.

Do You Have...

- Life insurance?
- Annuities?
- Long-term care insurance?
- Any passive income sources?
- Stock and bond portfolios?
- Liquid assets? (What's in your bank account?)
- Alternative investments?
- Rental properties?

---

[21] Amin Dabit. personalcapital.com. April 1, 2021. "The Average 401k Balance by Age." https://www.personalcapital.com/blog/retirement-planning/average-401k-balance-age/

If you are going through the work of sitting with a financial professional, it's important to look at your full retirement income picture and pull together *all* your assets, no matter how big or small. From the free insurance policy offered at your bank to the sizable investment in your brother-in-law's modestly successful furniture store, you want to have a good idea of where your money is.

One of the biggest challenges most retirees have at the beginning is this sense of being very overwhelmed. Before retirement, there are just a handful of critical bullet points clients need to check off to move toward their goals. Saving as much as they can, paying off debt, and taking advantage of tax breaks are just a few. Having things organized would be great, but I find most people are just too busy to dedicate any extra energy on top of saving as much as they can during their working years.

Launching into the retirement years, though, brings on a host of new bullet points, all of them critical. This is where being organized becomes very important. You need to know where things are, how those things work (at least at a basic level), and what you need for your lifestyle. This immediate demand for organization can really freak people out. They can become paralyzed and make no critical decisions out of a fear of making the wrong decision. It is very hard to get clarity on where you want to go if where you are now is a big messy pile of stuff.

Helping our new clients get organized is the first step of our Retirement Blueprint income and tax plan. Before any recommendations are made, first clarity needs to come on what our new client already has in motion. We take a detailed inventory of all assets, all income sources like pension and Social Security, the current tax structure of investments, and their current monthly lifestyle expenses. We even provide a nice, big organizational binder for our clients to store all their statements, tax documents, insurance documents, and reports. This gives organization not only to my clients, but also to my clients' beneficiaries. I tell my clients to let their kids know about this binder and where they can find it in the house. I've even added written instructions in the binder for the beneficiaries regarding what they should and should not do to avoid financial calamity if they're looking at the binder for the first time. I purposely made it kind of a stark white color binder so it sticks out and it's hopefully easy to find for a beneficiary.

Most of my new clients are surprised at just how much money they have once everything gets organized and put into one easy-to-read report, like a Retirement Blueprint. It is not uncommon for an individual to have five or six different retirement accounts, a couple of old 401(k)s at past employers, two bank accounts at separate banks, and maybe two or three non-retirement brokerage accounts. As of this writing, the state of Illinois is holding $3.5 billion in unclaimed (lost) funds for Illinoisans.[22] I believe the key reason for that is lack of organization. So, we get that fixed from the start.

Retirement Income Needs

How much income will you need in retirement? How do you determine that? A lot of people work toward a random number, thinking, "If I can just have a million dollars, I'll be comfortable in retirement!" Don't get me wrong; it is possible to save up a lot of money and then retire in the hopes you can keep your monthly expenses lower than some set estimation. But I think this carries a general risk of running out of money. Instead, I work with my clients to find out what their current and projected income needs are and then work from there to see how we might cover any gaps between what they have and what they want.

---

[22] Katy Smyser. NBC Chicago. April 26, 2022. "Unclaimed Money Illinois: Governments Could Owe You Money. Here's How to Claim It." https://www.nbcchicago.com/news/local/unclaimed-money-illinois-governments-could-owe-you-money-heres-how-to-claim-it/2816891

Goals and Dreams

I like to start with your pie in the sky. Do you find yourself planning for your vacations more thoroughly than you do your retirement? It's not uncommon for Americans to spend more time planning our vacations than we spend planning our retirements. Maybe it's because planning a vacation is less stressful: Having a week at the beach go awry is, well, a walk on the beach compared to running out of money in retirement. Whatever the case, perhaps it would be better if you thought of your retirement as a vacation in and of itself—no clocking in, no boss, no overtime. If you felt unlimited by financial strain, what would you do?

Would an endless vacation for you mean Paris and Rome? Would it mean mentoring at children's clubs or serving at the local soup kitchen? Or maybe it would mean deepening your ties to those immediately around you—neighbors, friends, and family. Maybe it would mean more time to take part in the hobbies and activities you love. Have you been considering a second (or even third) act as a small-business owner, turning a hobby or passion into a revenue source?

This is your time to daydream and answer the question: If you could do anything, what would you do?

After that, it's a matter of putting a dollar amount on it. What are the costs of round-the-world travel? One couple I know said their highest priority in retirement was being able to take each of their grandchildren on a cross-country vacation every year. That's a pretty specific goal—one that is reasonably easy to nail down expenses for.

A lot of people ask me what the most important thing is that they need to do to prepare for retirement. I believe the most important thing is not even financial: I believe it is knowing (or discovering) what you are passionate about doing besides work, and then finding out how you are going to implement that in retirement.

My clients Tom and Denice were passionate about moving to Florida once they were both retired. I guess they just had enough of the lovely winters we have here in Illinois. The problem was that two of their three kids were living in Illinois, along with four of the grandchildren, and the third child and grandchild number five were full-time residents of Florida. They did not want to create a family rift by moving residence from Illinois to Florida. They also felt that it was not financially feasible to have two houses. "Snow birding," or renting a place in Florida over the winter, was not the answer for them. It would be too long in between visits with the Illinois branch of the family. They were super passionate about this. Every meeting we had included a picture show of all the grandkids, especially the youngest in Florida, grandchild number five.

So, one of the Retirement Blueprint drafts that we put together was a scenario where they owned two homes for the next twenty years: one here in Illinois and one in Florida. Although it significantly increased their expenses over the twenty years, they did not run out of money. It may even turn out that they wind up with more money long term because of the equity growth in the new Florida house. It was engineered in a safe and secure fashion with proper bucket income planning.

Seeing the scenario in writing and explained by a professional was a game-changer for Tom and Denice. They acted almost immediately and within six months had closed on a new house in Fort Myers, Florida. They spend about a month in each location and still own both homes. The blessing here was their passion. They already knew exactly what they wanted to do and what was important to them about retirement. They just didn't know how to engineer it properly.

Current Expenses

Compiling a current expense report is one of the trickiest pieces of retirement preparation. Many people assume the expenses of their lives in retirement will be different—lower. After all, there will be no drive to work, no need for a formal wardrobe, and, perhaps most impactful of all, no more saving for retirement!

Yet, we often underestimate our daily spending habits. That's why I typically ask my clients to bring in their bank statements for the past year—they are reflective of your *actual* spending, not just what you think you're spending.

We don't use the "B" word in our office. What's the "B" word? "Budget." Nobody likes that word. I do not like that word. Instead, we use this word: "expense." More specifically, "monthly lifestyle expenses." What are your normal monthly lifestyle expenses? The two words couldn't be more different. Budget means fitting your monthly bills into some set income that cannot be altered by you. Being "on a budget" may mean that you cut down spending activities to fit into that set monthly cash flow coming in. It gives the connotation that what you want to live on is not in your control, but for some reason in some outside entity's control. Inherently, I feel the word "budget" is negative.

The word "expense" gives control back to you. Especially when you put the word lifestyle in front of it. Of course, some of your regular expenses are obligatory. You will have property tax payments, rent, utilities, groceries, fuel and transportation expenses, phone, etc. for the rest of your life.

But beyond those obligations, what is important to you about life that you really want to do? Travel? Golf? Vacation home? Spend more time with friends and family? We have had clients who wanted to open their own small business in retirement. I have another client who started their own small charity. Regardless, there's one thing that all of those activities have in common. They all cost money! And those expenses can be quantified into a typical annual, and then monthly, average expense.

I suggest a different approach when it comes to figuring out your monthly lifestyle expenses. Pretend for a moment that you have all the money you could ever want for all your dreams. Don't worry about how much that needs to be or how you'll get it. Let's just pretend you already have it. Now write down all your current obligation expenses in an itemized list. If you're unsure what they are, we would be happy to give you our monthly expense report worksheet as a guide. Now make sure you add the fun stuff, the lifestyle stuff. You're not just going to survive; you are going to live what you're passionate about. Focus on what your lifestyle expenses are today.

Do not worry about future inflation at this step. Just put down your expenses as if you were retiring today. Illustrating those expenses increasing with inflation over the years is what a good retirement income and tax planning software program should do for you, like a Retirement Blueprint, of course.

My bet is that your new monthly lifestyle expenses will be able to be engineered into your Retirement Blueprint with no problem. It is very, very rare that I meet someone who has a lifestyle expense so high that it cannot be engineered into the nest egg they have worked so hard to build. It does happen sometimes, but it is much more of a rarity. In fact, in many cases, it's just the opposite. So many times, I meet people who are reducing their lifestyle to try to "fit into their money," when just the opposite should be happening. They should be engineering their money properly to generate the monthly lifestyle expenses they desire.

I can't count the number of times I have sat with a couple, asked them about their spending, and heard them throw out a number that seemed incredibly low. When I ask them where the number came from, they usually say they estimated based on their total bills. Yet, our spending is so much more than our mortgage, utilities, cable, phone, car, grocery, or credit card bills.

"What about clothes?" I ask, "Or dining out? What about gifts and coffees and last-minute birthday cards?" That's when the lights come on.

This is why I suggest collecting a year's worth of information. There is usually no such thing as a one-time purchase. Did you buy new furniture? Even if that is a rarity, do you think that will be the last time you *ever* buy furniture?

One of my favorite parts of the Retirement Blueprint process is when a new client realizes the income plan is going to work and they are not going to run out of money. I think this is one of the most valuable reasons to work with a financial professional. My guess is most people who do it by themselves have a hard time believing what they're reading.

When I do meet someone who's put some effort in on their own creating an itemized list of monthly expenses, I find that they are ripping themselves off in most cases. They have all the survival and obligation expenses in there, but really no lifestyle expenses. A good financial professional can act as a reality coach and start adding in those lifestyle expenses to get a more accurate picture. Then they hold the hand of the client throughout the income planning process to illustrate how it is all going to work.

Another hefty expense is spending on the kids. Many of the couples I work with are quick to help their adult children, whether it's something like letting them live in the basement, paying for college, babysitting, paying an occasional bill, or contributing to a grandchild's college fund. Research concluded that 22 percent of adults receive some kind of financial support from parents. That segment jumps to almost 30 percent when factoring the generation we call millennials.[23]

My clients sometimes protest that what they do for their grown children can stop in retirement. They don't *need* to help. But I get it. Parents like to feel needed. And, while you never want to neglect saving for retirement in favor of taking on financial risks (like your child's student debt), the parents who help their adult children do so in part because it helps them feel fulfilled.

When it comes down to expenses, including (and especially) spending on your family, don't make your initial calculations based on what you *could* whittle your expenses down to if you *had* to. Instead, start from where you are. Who wants to live off a bare-bones bank account in retirement?

---

[23] Kamaron McNair. magnifymoney.com. October 26, 2021. "Nearly 30% of Millenials Still Receive Financial Support From Their Parents." https://www.magnifymoney.com/blog/news/parental-financial-support-survey

Other Expenses

Once you have nailed down your current expenses and your dreams or goals for retirement, there are a few other outstanding pieces to think about—some expenses many people don't take the time to consider before making and executing a plan. But I'm assuming you want to get it right, so let's take a look.

Housing

Do you know where you want to live in retirement? This makes up a substantial piece of your income puzzle—since the typical American household owns a home, and it's generally their largest asset.

Some people prefer to live right where they are for as long as they can. Others have been waiting for retirement to pull the trigger on an ambitious move, like purchasing a new house, or even downsizing. Whatever your plans and whatever your reasons, there are quite a few things to consider.

Mortgage
Do you still have a mortgage? What may have been a nice tax boon in your working years could turn into a financial burden in your retirement. After all, when you are on a limited income, a mortgage is just one more bill sapping your financial strength. It is something to put some thought into, whether you plan to age in place or are considering moving to your dream home, buying a house out of state, or living in a retirement community.

Upkeep and Taxes
A house without a mortgage still requires annual taxes. While it's tempting to think of this as a once-a-year expense, when you have limited earning potential, your annual tax bill might be something into which you should put a little more forethought.

The costs of homeownership aren't just monetary. When you find yourself dealing with more house than you need, it can drain your time and energy. From keeping clutter at bay to keeping the lawn mower running, upkeep can be extensive and expensive. For some, that's a challenge they heartily accept and can comfortably take on. For others, the idea of yard work or cleaning an area larger than they need feels foolish.

For instance, Peggy discovered after her knee replacement that most of her house was inaccessible to her when she was laid up.

"It felt ridiculous to pay someone else to dust and vacuum a house I was only living in 40 percent of!"

Practicality and Adaptability

Erik and Magda are looking to retire within the next two decades. They just sold their old three-bedroom ranch-style house. Their twins are in high school, and the couple has wanted to "upgrade" for years. Now they live in a gorgeous 1940s three-story house with all the kitchen space they ever wanted, five sprawling bedrooms, and a library and media room for themselves and their children. Within months of moving in, the couple realized a house perfect for their active teens would no longer be perfect for them in five to fifteen years.

"We are paying the mortgage for this house, but we've started saving for the next one," said Magda, "because who wants to climb two flights of stairs to their bedroom when they're seventy-eight?"

Others I know have encountered a similar situation in their personal lives. After a health crisis, one couple found the luxurious tub for two they toiled to install had become a specter of a bad slip and a potential safety risk. It's important to think through what your physical reality could be. I always emphasize to my clients that they should plan for whatever their long-term future might hold, but it's amazing how many people don't give it much thought.

Contracts and Regulations

If you are looking into a cross-country move, be aware of new tax tables or local ordinances in the area where you are looking to move. After all, you don't want to experience sticker-shock when you are looking at downsizing or reducing your bills in retirement.

Along the same lines, if you are moving into a retirement community, be sure to look at the fine print. What happens if you must move into a different situation for long-term care? Will you be penalized? Will you be responsible for replacing your slot in the community? What are all the fees, and what do they cover?

Inflation

As I write this in 2022, America has experienced a wave of inflation following a lengthy period of low inflation. Inflation zoomed to 8.5 percent in March 2022, a level not reached since 1981, and stood at 8.3 percent in April 2022.[24]

Core inflation is yet another measurement that excludes goods with prices that tend to be more volatile, such as food and energy costs. Core inflation for a 12-month period ending in April 2022 was 6.2 percent. It so happened energy prices rose a whopping 30.3 percent over that timeframe.[25]

However, inflation isn't a one-time bump; it has a cumulative effect. Again, that can impact the price of groceries greater than other goods. Even with relatively low inflation over the past few decades, an item you bought in 1997 for two dollars will cost

---

[24] tradingeconomics.com. April 2022. "United States Inflation Rate." https://tradingeconomics.com/united-states/inflation-cpi
[25] U.S. Inflation Calculator. "United States Core Inflation Rates (1957-2022)." https://www.usinflationcalculator.com/inflation/united-states-core-inflation-rates

$3.60 today.[26] Want to go to a show? A $20 ticket in 1997 would cost $40.34 in 2022.[27]

What if, in retirement, we hit a stretch like the late seventies and early eighties, when annual inflation rates of 10 percent became the norm? It may be wise to consider some extra padding in your retirement income plan to account for any potential increase in inflation in the future.

Aging

Also, in the expense category, think about longevity. We all hope to age gracefully. However, it's important to face the prospect of aging with a sense of realism.

The elephant in the room for many families is long-term care. No one wants to admit they will likely need it, but estimates indicate almost 70 percent of us will.[28] Aging is a significant piece of retirement income planning because you'll want to figure out how to set aside money for your care, either at home or away from it. The more comfortable you get with discussing your wishes and plans with your loved ones, the easier planning for the financial side of it can be.

I denote health care and potential long-term care costs in more detail elsewhere in this book, but suffice it to say nursing home care tends to be very expensive and typically isn't something you get to choose when you will need.

It isn't just the costs of long-term care that pose a concern in living longer. It's also about covering the possible costs of everything else associated with living longer. For instance, if Henry retires from his job as a biochemical engineer at age sixty-five, perhaps he planned to have a very decent income for twenty

---

[26] Ibid.

[27] In2013dollars.com "Admission to movies, theaters, and concerts priced at $20 in 1997>$40.34 in 2022." https://www.in2013dollars.com/Admission-to-movies,-theaters,-and-concerts/price-inflation

[28] Moll Law Group. 2022. "The Cost of Long-Term Care."
https://www.molllawgroup.com/the-cost-of-long-term-care.html

years, until age eighty-five. But what if he lives until he's ninety-five? That's a whole third—ten years—more of personal income he will need.

Putting It All Together

Whew! So, you have pulled together what you have, and you have a pretty good idea of where you want to be. Now your financial professional and you can go about the work of arranging what assets you *have* to cover what you *need*—and how you might try to cover any gaps.

Like the proverbial man in the Bible who built his house on a rock, I like to help my clients figure out how to cover their day-to-day living expenses—their needs—with insurance and other guaranteed income sources like pensions and Social Security.

There are two main reasons someone hires us to do a Retirement Blueprint. They are either concerned about running out of money in retirement, or they are concerned about taxes for themselves or their family.

As I mentioned earlier, the first step of our Retirement Blueprint process is to get clarity on where our new client is today. We gather all statements, tax returns, insurance, and expense reports. All that data is input into our Retirement Blueprint software. The program will illustrate those monthly expenses increasing over the retirement years with an inflation rate of the client's choosing. In that first scenario, before any recommendations are made, the program helps answer the number one question most retirees have: "If I continue on the same financial course, am I going to run out of money in retirement?"

In many cases, the program does show the client running out of money at some point in this first scenario. Maybe it illustrates that happening at age 115, or maybe it illustrates that nightmare scenario at age eighty. The main culprit here? Inflation. The biggest error I see with people who do their own, homegrown retirement income plans is that they do not account very well for inflation. Absolutely you will be spending more on your lifestyle expenses in ten years, and if your money is not keeping pace with that inflation, it will run down. It could be a situation where the client does not run out of money but is concerned with running the value down below a level they are comfortable with. Or they could be concerned about just how their investments are going to produce the income needed, or that the probability of success with the current investment choices is very low due to market volatility. Regardless, the next two steps of Retirement Blueprint are focused on how to fix these situations.

The Emergency Account Bucket

I suggest six months of expenses (including fun lifestyle) should be in cash at the bank in a savings account. For instance, if you have a normal monthly lifestyle expense of $6,000 per month, that is $72,000 per year. So, you should have $36,000 in cash at the bank. I would round up to the next $10,000 increment. So, in this case, $40,000 is what I would suggest being in the emergency account. A good rule of thumb here is if you wanted to go buy a car and put down 50 percent of the cost of the car with a personal check, you shouldn't have to call me first. Just write the check. Sometimes people will say, "Well, Ed, that's a lot of money to have sitting in a savings account earning almost nothing." Yes, it is. But that is not the point of what this money is there for. This money needs to be liquid to you at a moment's notice with no tax consequences and no penalties for you to use it. Rate of return is not the most important thing with your emergency account.

The Income Bucket

Once we've gone through that first scenario, we get into the planning and recommendations. The first thing we look at is Social Security and maximizing those choices for income and taxes (more about that later). We do the same for any pensions the client has coming. Once we have a strong feeling about what we believe the client will get from Social Security and pension and we have confirmed their probable monthly lifestyle expenses, we discover what the gap is between those two numbers. That gap becomes the target number for the entire Income Bucket. It is a number that moves with inflation and will also change because of life. Health insurance premiums will change or completely disappear at age sixty-five because of Medicare, but new expenses will come online like Medicare Supplements. Cars will be purchased. Cars will be sold. Travel expenses might be heavier in the first ten years of retirement, a little less in the next ten years, and then completely dissipate in the next ten. We attempt to get a very accurate target of what our clients are going to need to withdraw out of their investments to cover the gap. It then just becomes a matter of finding the right products or investments that have the highest probability of producing that income gap for the client with the lowest amount of risk.

The Growth Bucket

The next step is for the remaining assets (not allocated into the income or emergency buckets) to be invested in a long-term growth strategy that makes sense for the client in terms of time horizon and risk tolerance. I am comfortable with clients taking a moderate level of risk dependent on the opportunity. However, any money in this bucket is intended as a long-term investment. Usually, investment recommendations here are completely liquid and have no time commitment, but investors should realize that the bulk of the money will need to stay in this bucket for five to ten years to deal with different market conditions and corrections. Maybe even a bear market. Therefore, I suggest a diversified portfolio in the Growth Bucket. This not only diversifies how the client is making money but hopefully diversifies when bad things happen in a given market. If you're exposed just to one market type, that means that the bad thing happens to all the growth money all at the same time. But if you are exposed to different market types, perhaps when a bad thing happens in one market, the other market does not experience the bad thing. In some cases, when a bad thing happens in one market, another market prospers!

Tax Planning

The final part of the Retirement Blueprint is the tax plan. This is the portion of our planning process that never ends. The Income Bucket, Growth Bucket, and Emergency Account Bucket are all things that can be set up in the first year of working with a new client. Adjustments might need to be made from year to year, but it is likely that it is just an allocation change inside the same portfolio to take advantage of or defend from market conditions. This is not the case with tax planning. It is constantly changing. The government changes the rules regularly. On top of that, our clients often change their minds on their goals and what they want to see happen with their money. This causes shifts in the Retirement Blueprint, and the biggest impact usually is taxes. Plus, we usually have some kind of multi-year Roth conversion plan, and that is adjusting every year. More about that later.

Annual Review and Strategy Meetings

As you have probably guessed from the last few paragraphs, the Retirement Blueprint needs regular adjustment. This would be like sailing a ship across the ocean from New York to London. At the beginning of the journey, you have a set course you plan on following to get from point A to point B. Along the way, you need to make course corrections due to weather, icebergs, and other ships. If you do not adjust the course regularly, you will probably never get to London in the best case; in the worst case, you sink.

Again, you should keep in mind there isn't one single financial vehicle, asset, or source to fill all your needs, and that's okay. One of the challenges of planning for your income in retirement concerns figuring out what products and strategies to use. You can release some of that stress when you accept the fact you will probably need a diverse portfolio—potentially with bonds, stocks, insurance, and other income sources—not just one massive money pile.

One way to help shore up your income gaps is by working with your financial professional and a qualified tax advisor to mitigate your tax exposure. If you have a 401(k) or IRA, a tax advisor in your corner can help you figure out how and when to take distributions from your account in a way that doesn't push you into a higher tax bracket. Or you might learn how to use tax-advantaged bonds more effectively. Effective tax planning isn't necessarily about "adding" to your income. Especially regarding retirement, it's less about what you make than it is about what you keep. Paying a lower tax bill keeps more money in your pocket, which is where you want it when it comes to retirement income.

Now you can look at ways to cover your remaining retirement goals. Are there products like long-term care insurance specific to a certain kind of expense you anticipate? Is there a particular asset you want to use for your "play" money—money for trips and gifts for the grandkids? Is there any way you can portion off money for those charitable legacy plans?

Once you have analyzed your income wants, needs, and the assets to realistically cover them, you may have a gap. The masterstroke of a competent financial professional will be to help you figure out how you will cover that gap. Will you need to cut out a round of golf a week? Maybe skip the new car? Or will you need to take more substantial action?

One way to cover an income gap is to consider working longer or even part-time before retirement and even after that magical calendar date. This may not be the best "plan" for you; disabilities, work demands, and physical or emotional limitations can hinder the best-laid plans to continue working. However, if it is physically possible for you, this is one considerable way to help your assets last, for more than one reason.

In fact, 46 percent of the Americans responding to a survey report they plan to work part-time after retiring, while 18 percent indicated they planned to work past the age of seventy.[29]

Mark hated his job. When we started working together, he specifically asked to meet me in the morning before he went to work or on a day off because he was usually so unhappy and angry by the end of a typical workday. He was only fifty-five years old when we first met, and he just assumed he'd have to wait until age fifty-nine and a half at the earliest to start using some of his retirement money without IRS penalty. Plus, the earliest he could start his Social Security was age sixty-two, and what about health insurance? Medicare doesn't start until age sixty-five. You could just see the stress on Mark's face when we talked about this. His youngest child at that point was fifteen, and Mark intended on paying for her college. That was the commitment that kept him a slave to this thing he hated.

I knew when we were still in the beginning meeting with Mark that I'd be able to help engineer his early retirement. It was really a math problem more than anything else. For sure, his expenses would be higher in the first few years of retirement and a significant portion of his nest egg would need to go toward these expenses, but things would level out by the time he was sixty-five. Plus, there are solutions that allow people to access qualified retirement funds before age fifty-nine and a half. They are called 72(t) withdrawals.[30] They are not for everybody, and they come with IRS obligations, but it is a tool that could be used for early retirement.

We carefully went through Mark's Retirement Blueprint together and got to the point where Mark realized he would be

---

[29] Palash Ghosh. Forbes.com. May 6, 2021. "A Third Of Seniors Seek To Work Well Past Retirement Age, Or Won't Retire At All, Poll Finds." https://www.forbes.com/sites/palashghosh/2021/05/06/a-third-of-seniors-seek-to-work-well-past-retirement-age-or-wont-retire-at-all-poll-finds/?sh=1d2ece836b95
[30] Julia Kagan. Investopedia. June 17, 2021. "Rule 72(t)." https://www.investopedia.com/terms/r/rule72t.asp

able to retire immediately if he wanted—even with the added expense of his daughter's college. His entire demeanor changed. You could see the concerns dissipate. Surprisingly, he decided to keep working. Mark told me at our first annual review that knowing he could walk out the door at any moment and never come back was a complete mental shift for him with work (Mark's actual words about what he felt he could say to his employers while walking out the door are not printable). He started taking off early to meet me in the afternoon for review meetings! He did finally retire at sixty and is doing great today.

CHAPTER 5

Social Security

S ocial Security is often the foundation of retirement income. Backed by the strength of the U.S. Treasury, it provides perhaps the most dependable paycheck you will have in retirement.

From the time you collect your first paycheck from the job that made you a bonafide taxpayer, you are paying into the grand old Social Security system. What grew and developed out of the pressures of the Great Depression has become one of the most popular government programs in the country, and, if you pay in for the equivalent of ten years or more, you, too, can benefit from the Social Security program.

Now, before we get into the nitty-gritty of Social Security, I'd like to address a current concern: Will Social Security still be there for you when you reach retirement age?

The Future of Social Security

This question is ever-present as headlines trumpet an underfunded Social Security program, alongside the sea of baby boomers retiring in droves and the comparatively smaller pool of younger people who are funding the system.

The Social Security Administration itself acknowledges this concern as each Social Security statement now bears an asterisk that continues near the end of the summary:

*"*Your estimated benefits are based on current law. Congress has made changes to the law in the past and can do so at any time. The law governing benefit amounts may change because, by 2034, the payroll taxes collected will be enough to pay only about 79 percent of scheduled benefits."*

Just a reminder, as if you needed one, that nothing in life is guaranteed. Additionally, depending on who you're listening to, Social Security funds may run low before 2034 thanks to the financial instability and government spending that accompanied the 2020 COVID-19 pandemic.

Before you get too discouraged, though, here are a few thoughts to keep you going:

- Even if the program is only paying 79 cents on the dollar for scheduled benefits, 79 percent is notably not zero.
- The Social Security Administration has made changes in the distant and near past to protect the fund's solvency, including increasing retirement ages and striking certain filing strategies.
- There are many changes Congress could make, and lawmakers routinely discuss how to fix the system, such as further increasing full retirement age and eligibility.
- One thing no one is seriously discussing? Reneging on current obligations to retirees or the soon-to-retire.

Take heart. The real answer to the question, "Will Social Security be there for me?" is still yes.

This question is important to consider when you look at how much we, as a nation, rely on this program. Did you know Social Security benefits replace about 40 percent of a person's original income when they retire?[31]

---

[31] ssa.gov. "Alternate Measure of Replacement Rates for Social Security Benefits and Retirement Income."
https://www.ssa.gov/policy/docs/ssb/v68n2/v68n2p1.html

If you ask me, that's a pretty significant piece of your retirement income puzzle.

Another caveat? You may not realize this, but no one can legally "advise" you about your Social Security benefits.

"But, Ed," you may be thinking, "isn't that part of what you do? And what about that nice gentleman at the Social Security Administration office I spoke with on the phone?"

Don't get me wrong. Social Security Administration employees know their stuff. They are trained to understand policies and programs, and they are usually pretty quick to tell you what you can and cannot do. But the government specifically stipulates, because Social Security is a benefit you alone have paid into and earned, your Social Security decisions, too, are yours alone.

When it comes to financial professionals, we can't push you in any direction, but—there's a big but here—working with a well-informed financial professional is still incredibly handy for your Social Security decisions. Why? Because someone who's worth his or her salt will know what withdrawal strategies might pertain to your specific situation and will ask questions that can help you determine what you are looking for when it comes to your Social Security.

For instance, some people want the highest possible monthly benefit. Others want to start their benefits early, not always because of financial need. I heard about one man who called in to start his Social Security payments the day he qualified, just because he liked to think of it as the government paying back a debt it owed him, and he enjoyed the feeling of receiving a check from Uncle Sam.

Whatever your reasons, questions, or feelings regarding Social Security, the decision is yours alone; but working with a financial professional can help you put your options in perspective by showing you—both with industry knowledge and with proprietary software or planning processes—where your benefits fit into your overall strategy for retirement income.

One reason the federal government doesn't allow for "advice" related to Social Security, I suspect, is so no one can profit from giving you advice related to your Social Security benefit—or from providing any clarifications. Again, this is a sign of a good financial professional. Those who are passionate about their work will be knowledgeable about what benefit strategies might be to your advantage and will happily share those possible options with you.

Full Retirement Age

When it comes to Social Security, it seems like many people only think so far as "yes." They don't take the time to understand the various options available. Instead, because it is common knowledge you can begin your benefits at age sixty-two, that's what many of us do. While more people are opting to delay taking benefits, age sixty-two is still firmly the most popular age to start.[32]

What many people fail to understand is, by starting benefits early, they may be leaving a lot of money on the table. You see, the Social Security Administration bases your monthly benefit on two factors: your earnings history and your full retirement age (FRA).

From your earnings history, they pull the thirty-five years you made the most money and use a mathematical indexing formula to figure out a monthly average from those years. If you paid into the system for less than thirty-five years, then every year you didn't pay in will be counted as a zero.

Once they have calculated what your monthly earning would be at FRA, the government then calculates what to put on your check based on how close you are to FRA. FRA was originally set at sixty-five, but, as the population aged and lifespans lengthened, the government shifted FRA later and later, based on an

---

[32] Chris Kissell. moneytalknews.com. January 20, 2021. "This Is When the Most People Start Taking Social Security." https://www.moneytalksnews.com/the-most-popular-age-for-claiming-social-security

individual's year of birth. Check out the following chart to see when you will reach FRA.[33]

Age to Receive Full Social Security Benefits*	
(Called "full retirement age" [FRA] or "normal retirement age.")	
Year of Birth*	**FRA**
1937 or earlier	65
1938	65 and 2 months
1939	65 and 4 months
1940	65 and 6 months
1941	65 and 8 months
1942	65 and 10 months
1943-1954	66
1955	66 and 2 months
1956	66 and 4 months
1957	66 and 6 months
1958	66 and 8 months
1959	66 and 10 months
1960 and later	67
*If you were born on Jan. 1 of any year, you should refer to the previous year. (If you were born on the 1st of the month, we figure your benefit [and your full retirement age] as if your birthday was in the previous month.)	

[33] Social Security Administration. "Full Retirement Age." https://www.ssa.gov/planners/retire/retirechart.html

When you reach FRA, you are eligible to receive 100 percent of whatever the Social Security Administration says is your full monthly benefit.

Starting at age sixty-two, for every year before FRA you claim benefits, your monthly check is reduced by 5 percent or more. Conversely, for every year you delay taking benefits past FRA, your monthly benefit increases by 8 percent (until age seventy—after that, there is no monetary advantage to delaying Social Security benefits). While your circumstances and needs may vary, a lot of financial professionals still urge people to at least consider delaying until they reach age seventy.

Why wait?[34]

Taking benefits early could affect your monthly check by ___.								
62	63	64	65	FRA 66	67	68	69	70
-25%	-20%	-13.3%	-6.7%	0	+8%	+16%	+24%	+32%

My Social Security

If you are over age thirty, you have probably received a notice from the Social Security Administration telling you to activate something called "My Social Security." This is a handy way to learn more about your particular benefit options, to keep track of what your earnings record looks like, and to calculate the benefits you have accrued over the years.

Essentially, My Social Security is an online account you can activate to see what your personal Social Security picture looks like, which you can do at www.ssa.gov/myaccount. This can be extremely helpful when it comes to planning for income in retirement and figuring up the difference between your anticipated income versus anticipated expenses.

---

[34] Social Security Administration. April 2021. "Can You Take Your Benefits Before Full Retirement Age?"
https://www.ssa.gov/planners/retire/applying2.html

My Social Security is also helpful because it's a great way to see if there is a problem. For instance, I have heard of one woman who, through diligently checking her tax records against her Social Security profile, discovered her Social Security check was shortchanging her, based on her earnings history. After taking the discrepancy to the Social Security Administration, they sent her what they owed her in makeup benefits.

COLA

Social Security is a largely guaranteed piece of the retirement puzzle: If you get a statement that reads you should expect $1,000 a month, you can be sure you will receive $1,000 a month. But there is one variable detail, and that is something called the cost-of-living adjustment, or COLA.

The COLA is an increase in your monthly check meant to address inflation in everyday life. After all, your expenses will likely continue to experience inflation in retirement, but you will no longer have the opportunity for raises, bonuses, or promotions you had when you were working. Instead, Social Security receives an annual cost-of-living increase tied to the Department of Labor's Consumer Price Index for Urban Wage Earners and Clerical Workers, or CPI-W. If the CPI-W measurement shows inflation rose a certain amount for regular goods and services, then Social Security recipients will see that reflected in their COLA.

The COLA averages 4 percent, but in a no- or low-inflation environment, such as in 2010, 2011, and 2016, Social Security recipients will not receive an adjustment. Some view the COLA as a perk, bump, or bonus, but, in reality, it works more like this: Your mom sends you to the store with $2.50 for a gallon of milk. Milk costs exactly $2.50. The next week, you go back with that same amount, but it is now $2.52 for a gallon, so you go back to Mom, and she gives you 2 cents. You aren't bringing home more milk—it just costs more money.

So the COLA is less about "making more money" and more about keeping seniors' purchasing power from eroding when inflation is a big factor, such as in 1975, when it was 8 percent![35] Still, don't let that detract from your enthusiasm about COLAs; after all, what if Mom's solution was: "Here's the same $2.50; try to find pennies from somewhere else to get that milk!"?

Spousal Benefits

We've talked about FRA, but another big Social Security decision involves spousal benefits.

If you or your spouse has a long stretch of zeros in your earnings history—perhaps if one of you stayed home for years, caring for children or sick relatives—you may want to consider filing for spousal benefits instead of filing on your own earnings history. A spousal benefit can be up to 50 percent of the primary wage earner's benefit at full retirement age.

To begin drawing a spousal benefit, you must be at least sixty-two years old, and the primary wage earner must have already filed for his or her benefit. While there are penalties for taking spousal benefits early (you could lose up to 67.5 percent of your check for filing at age sixty-two), you cannot earn credits for delaying past full retirement age.[36]

Like I wrote, the spousal benefit can be a big deal for those who don't have a very long pay history, but it's important to weigh your own earned benefits against the option of withdrawing based on a fraction of your spouse's benefits.

To look at how this could play out, let's use a hypothetical couple: Mary Jane, who is sixty, and Peter, who is sixty-two.

Let's say Peter's benefit at FRA, in his case sixty-six, would be $1,600. If Peter begins his benefits right now, four years before

---

[35] Social Security Administration. "Cost-Of-Living Adjustment (COLA) Information for 2022." https://www.ssa.gov/cola

[36] Social Security Administration. "Retirement Planner: Benefits For You As A Spouse." https://www.ssa.gov/planners/retire/applying6.html

FRA, his monthly check will be $1,200. If Mary Jane begins taking spousal benefits in two years at the earliest date possible, her monthly benefits will be reduced by 67.5 percent, to $520 per month (remember, at FRA, the most she can qualify for is half of Peter's FRA benefit).

What if Peter and Mary Jane both wait until FRA? At sixty-six, Peter begins taking his full benefit of $1,600 a month. Two years later, when she reaches age sixty-six, Mary Jane will qualify for $800 a month. By waiting until FRA, the couple's monthly benefit goes from $1,720 to $2,400.

What if Peter delays until age seventy to get his maximum possible benefit? For each year past FRA he delays, his monthly benefits increase by 8 percent. This means, at seventy, he could file for a monthly benefit of $2,176. However, delayed retirement credits do not affect spousal benefits, so as soon as Peter files at seventy, Mary Jane would also file (at age sixty-eight) for her maximum benefit of $800, so their highest possible combined monthly check is $2,976.[37]

When it comes to your Social Security benefits, you obviously will want to consider whether a monthly check based on a fraction of your spouse's earnings will be comparable to or larger than your own earnings history.

Divorced Spouses

There are a few considerations for those of us who have gone through a divorce. If you 1) were married for ten years or more *and* 2) have since been divorced for at least two years *and* 3) are unmarried *and* 4) your ex-spouse qualifies to begin Social Security, you qualify for a spousal benefit based on your ex-husband or ex-wife's earnings history at FRA. A divorced spousal benefit is different from the married spousal benefit in one way:

---

[37] Office of the Chief Actuary. Social Security Administration. "Social Security Benefits: Benefits for Spouses."
https://www.ssa.gov/oact/quickcalc/spouse.html

You don't have to wait for your ex-spouse to file before you can file yourself.[38]

For instance, Charles and Moira were married for fifteen years before their divorce, when he was thirty-six and she was forty. Moira has been remarried for twenty years, and, although Charles briefly remarried, his second marriage ended after a few years. Charles' benefits are largely calculated based on his many years of volunteering in schools, meaning his personal monthly benefit is close to zero.

Although Moira has deferred her retirement, opting to delay benefits until she is seventy, Charles can begin taking benefits calculated from Moira's work history at FRA as early as sixty-two. However, he will also have the option of waiting until FRA to collect the maximum, or 50 percent of Moira's earned monthly benefit at her FRA.

Widowed Spouses

If your marriage ended with the death of your spouse, you might claim a benefit for your spouse's earned income as his or her widow/widower, called a survivor's benefit. Unlike a spousal benefit or divorced benefits, if your husband or wife dies, you can claim his or her full benefit. Also, unlike spousal benefits, if you need to, you can begin taking income when you turn sixty. However, as with other benefit options, your monthly check will be permanently reduced for withdrawing benefits before FRA.

If your spouse began taking benefits before he or she died, you can't delay withdrawing your survivor's benefits to get delayed credits. The Social Security Administration maintains you can

---

[38] Social Security Administration. "Retirement Planner: If You Are Divorced." https://www.ssa.gov/planners/retire/divspouse.html

only get as much from a survivor's benefit as your deceased spouse might have received, had he or she lived.[39]

Taxes, Taxes, Taxes

With Social Security, as with everything, it is important to consider taxes. It may be surprising, but your Social Security benefits are not tax-free. Despite having been taxed to accrue those benefits in the first place, you may have to pay Uncle Sam income taxes on up to 85 percent of your Social Security.

The Social Security Administration figures these taxes using what they call "the provisional income formula." Your provisional income formula differs from the adjusted gross income you use for your regular income taxes. Instead, to find out how much of your Social Security benefit is taxable, the Social Security Administration calculates it this way:

Provisional Income = Adjusted Gross Income + Nontaxable Interest + ½ of Social Security

See that piece about nontaxable interest? That generally means interest from government bonds and notes. It surprises many people that, although you may not pay taxes on those assets, their income will count against you when it comes to Social Security taxation.

Once you have figured out your provisional income (also called "combined income"), you can use the following chart to figure out your Social Security taxes.[40]

---

[39] Social Security Administration. "Social Security Benefit Amounts For The Surviving Spouse By Year Of Birth."
https://www.ssa.gov/planners/survivors/survivorchartred.html
[40] Social Security Administration. "Benefits Planner: Income Taxes and Your Social Security Benefits." https://www.ssa.gov/planners/taxes.html

Taxes on Social Security		
Provisional Income = Adjusted Gross Income + Nontaxable Interest + ½ of Social Security		
If you are __ and your provisional income is__, then...		Uncle Sam will tax __ of your Social Security
Single	Married, filing jointly	
Less than $25,000	Less than $32,000	0%
$25,000 to $34,000	$32,000 to $44,000	Up to 50%
More than $34,000	More than $44,000	Up to 85%

This is one more reason it may benefit you to work with financial and tax professionals. They can look at your entire financial picture to make your overall retirement plan as tax-efficient as possible—including your Social Security benefit.

A big item we promote to our clients is understanding the tax efficiency of Social Security income. As stated above, if all the income you have in the world is just your Social Security, you will pay no federal income tax on it! Even if it turns out that your Social Security is going to be taxable, the maximum is 85 percent. So that means you will get 15 percent tax-free for sure. It is one of the most tax-efficient parts of your retirement income.

With that said, we try to use the Social Security income as a strategic tax-free source of income for at least the early years of our clients' retirements. This could open new opportunities for our clients, like Roth conversions. In a perfect world, we would like to see our clients get the deduction of their 401(k) and IRA contributions in their working years, and then do Roth conversions after retirement at a lower tax bracket (hopefully). Of course, that doesn't work for everyone. However, the fact that a portion or all of your Social Security income could be coming to you tax-free opens the opportunity for that type of planning.

Working and Social Security: The Earnings Test

If you haven't reached FRA, but you started your Social Security benefits and are still working, things get a little hairy.

Because you have started Social Security payments, the Social Security Administration will pay out your benefits (at that reduced rate, of course, because you haven't reached your FRA). Yet, because you are working, the organization must also withhold from your check to add to your benefits, which you are already collecting. See how this complicates matters?

To address the situation, the government has what is called the earnings test. For 2022, you can earn up to $19,560 without it affecting your Social Security check. But, for every $2 you earn past that amount, the Social Security Administration will withhold $1. The earnings test loosens in the year of your FRA; if you are reaching FRA in 2022, you can earn up to $51,960 before you run into the earnings test, and the government only withholds $1 for every $3 past that amount. The month you reach FRA, you are no longer subject to any earnings withholding. For instance, if you are still working and will turn sixty-six on December 28, 2022, you would only have to worry about the earnings test until December, and then you can ignore it entirely. Keep in mind, the money the government withholds from your Social Security benefits while you are working before FRA will be tacked back onto your benefits check after FRA.[41]

As I mentioned before, your Social Security income is a big part of your retirement income and tax plan. In many cases, we find that with good Social Security claiming strategies, the amount our clients will get from Social Security may be much higher than initially thought before the planning. This is especially true for our married clients making smart claiming choices that support

---

[41] Social Security Administration. "Exempt Amounts Under the Earnings Test." https://www.ssa.gov/oact/cola/rtea.html

each other. Of course, all of this is dependent on Social Security following through with the commitments they made to our clients, but it is not my opinion that Social Security could completely fail. It may turn out that my clients' payments are lower than anticipated due to Social Security solvency changes, but they won't go away. If that dreadful thing were to happen, really smart scenario planning becomes even more important.

I have had situations where a client thought they did not have enough money saved up for retirement, but after we did some solid Social Security scenario planning, they discovered the probable income from Social Security would be much higher. This meant that Social Security covered much more of their income than initially first thought. This then meant that they did not need as much nest egg money to generate the gap between their Social Security and lifestyle expenses. In those cases, it is not uncommon for clients to go from not having enough money to having plenty of money to retire.

It is the power of making those smart choices to maximize the income, combined with the fact that Social Security can be partially or completely tax-free income to my clients, that make it probably the most powerful planning lever in the retiree's toolbox.

CHAPTER 6

401(k)s & IRAs

Have you heard? Today's retirement is not your parents' retirement. You see, back in the day, it was pretty common to work for one company for the vast majority of your career and then retire with a gold watch and a pension.

The gold watch was a symbol of the quality time you had put in at that company, but the pension was more than a symbol. Instead, it was a guarantee—as solid as your employer—that they would repay your hard work with a certain amount of income in your old age. Did you see the caveat there? Your pension's guarantee was *as solid as your employer.* The problem was, what if your employer went under?

Companies that failed couldn't pay their retired employees' pensions, leading to financial challenges for many. Beginning in 1974 with Congress' passage of the Employee Retirement Income Security Act, federal legislation and regulations aimed at protecting retirees were everywhere. One piece of legislation included a relatively obscure section of the Internal Revenue Code, added in 1978. Section 401(k), to be specific.

IRC section 401, subsection k, created tax advantages for employer-sponsored financial products, even if the main contributor was the employee him or herself. Over the years, more employers took note, beginning an age of transition away from pensions and toward 401(k) plans. A 401(k) is a retirement account with certain tax benefits and restrictions on the investments or other financial products inside of it.

Essentially, 401(k)s and their individual retirement account (IRA) counterparts are "wrappers" that provide tax benefits around assets; typically, the assets that compose IRAs and 401(k)s are mutual funds, stock and bond mixes, and money market accounts. However, IRA and 401(k) contents are becoming more diverse these days, with some companies offering different kinds of annuity options within their plans.

Where pensions are defined-*benefit* plans, 401(k)s and IRAs are defined-*contribution* plans. The one-word change outlines the basic difference. Pensions spell out what you can expect to receive from the plan but not necessarily how much money it will take to fund those benefits. With 401(k)s, an employer sets a standard for how much they will contribute (if any), and you can be certain of what you are contributing. Still, there is no outline for what you can expect to receive in return for those contributions.

Modern employment looks very different. A 2020 survey by the Bureau of Labor Statistics determined U.S. workers stayed with their employers a median of 4.1 years. Workers ages fifty-five to sixty-four had a little more staying power and were most likely to stay with their employer for about ten years.[42] Participation in 401(k) plans has steadily risen this century, totaling $7.3 trillion in assets in 2021 compared to $3.1 trillion in 2011. About 60 million active participants engaged in 401(k) plans in 2020.[43]

Those statistics make it clear that 401(k) plans have replaced pensions at many companies and, for that matter, a gold watch.

What do you think is the biggest difference is between the generation retiring now compared to previous generations?

---

[42] Bureau of Labor Statistics. September 22, 2020. "Employee Tenure Summary." https://www.bls.gov/news.release/tenure.nr0.htm
[43] Investment Company Institute. October 11, 2021. "Frequently Asked Questions About 401(k) Plan Research." https://www.ici.org/faqs/faq/401k/faqs_401k

Based on my thirty-year career, the biggest difference I see is that current generations are retiring without pensions. Think about your mom or your dad (or maybe your grandma and grandpa) and their retirement years. Odds are, they probably retired with some type of pension. That, combined with their Social Security, gave them a comfortable and safe retirement income.

However, nowadays a new client having a pension is more of a rarity, unless they are a government or union employee. We do not have the income safety or guarantees that our parents' generation had. Instead, we have a pile of money in our 401(k) or IRA. Our employers figured out many years ago that they could not mathematically afford to support workers guaranteed income throughout retirement as life expectancy increased. They realized their pensions would go bankrupt (government and union pensions will figure this out soon–the hard way). Therefore, they changed their retirement benefit programs from defined benefit plans (guaranteed pension) to defined contribution plans (401(k)s). In a nutshell, Corporate America shifted all the risk of planning to have enough income in retirement from the company over to you, the employee.

While we are in our working years, or the accumulation phase, this seems pretty good! We see our savings and our employers' contributions build up in our 401(k). According to Vanguard, the average 401(k) balance for those actually participating in a 401(k) at age sixty-five was $255,151 in 2021.[44] In a household with two workers, that would be over $500,000! A ton more in ratio than our grandparents had saved up at sixty-five. That is because there were no contributions being made by employers into our grandparent's retirement programs. All that money went into their defined benefit pension programs.

But when we get to retirement, the income phase, and want to have income we can count on, our grandparents' situation looks

---

[44]Vanguard. June 2021. "How America Saves 2021." https://institutional.vanguard.com/content/dam/inst/vanguard-has/insights-pdfs/21_CIR_HAS21_HAS_FSreport.pdf

pretty good. Granted, they probably had significantly less money in retirement savings, but they had these guaranteed pension payments on top of their Social Security they could count on for the rest of their lives. In many cases, those pension payments would continue for their spouses if they died. It brought a sense of security. It also brought lifestyle. They could vacation, buy a little cottage, get a new car every five years, and in general, do the things they always wanted to because they knew the income would be there to pay the bills.

Sounds pretty good, doesn't it? I find that this is what most of my clients desire. They want a pension-like feel with the money they have worked so hard to save. They want what their grandparents had, but also want to still control and grow their money. They to have their cake and eat it too. So, for many of our new clients, this is one of the first things we help them engineer to guarantee pension-like income off retirement savings and still maintain control of assets.

If there is anything to learn from this paradigm shift, it's that you must look out for yourself. Whether you have worked for a company for two years or twenty, you are still the one who has to look out for your own best interests. That holds doubly true when it comes to preparing for retirement. If you are one of the lucky ones who still has a pension, good for you. But for the rest of us, it is likely a 401(k)—or possibly one of its nonprofit- or government-sector counterparts, a 403(b) or 457 plan—is one of your biggest assets for retirement.

Some employers offer incentives to contribute to their company plans, like a company match. On that subject, I have one thing to say: *Do it!* Nothing in life is free, as they say, but a company match on your retirement funds is about as close to free money as it gets. If you can make the minimum to qualify for your company's match at all, go for it.

Now, it's likely, during our working years, we mostly "set and forget" our 401(k) funding. Because it is tax-advantaged, your employer is taking money from your paycheck—before taxes— and putting it into your plan for you. Maybe you got to pick a selection of investments, or maybe your company only offers one choice of investment in your 401(k). Either way, while you are gainfully employed, your most impactful decision may just be the decision to continue funding your plan in the first place. But, when you are ready to retire or move jobs, you have choices to make requiring a little more thought and care.

When you are ready to part ways with your job, you have a few options:

- Leave the money where it is
- Take the cash (and pay income taxes and perhaps a 10 percent additional federal tax if you are younger than age fifty-nine-and-one-half)
- Transfer the money to another employer plan (if the new plan allows)
- Roll the money over into a self-directed IRA

Now, these are just general options. You will have to decide, hopefully with the help of a financial professional, what's right for you. For instance, 401(k)s are typically pretty closely tied to the companies offering them, so when changing jobs, it may not always be possible to transfer a 401(k) to another 401(k). Leaving the money where it is may also be out of the question— some companies have direct cash payout or rollover policies once someone is no longer employed.

Also, remember what we mentioned earlier about how we change jobs more often these days? That means you likely have a 401(k) with your current company, but you may also have a string of retirement accounts trailing you from other jobs.

We live in an age where the typical worker will have over ten jobs in their career. If you have a spouse, that's twenty jobs for your household. That's twenty possible 401(k)s scattered all over the place. No wonder people can feel lost and like they don't have enough money to retire if they have to go through twenty statements just to get a value of where they're at today. However, you can combine all those old 401(k)s together into your own traditional IRA account. There are no taxes or penalties to do that, regardless of your age. Most of the larger brokerage firms (T.D. Ameritrade, Fidelity, Charles Schwab, etc.) will allow you to open a new IRA account for free. I highly suggest, from an organizational standpoint if nothing else, that you do this. I also suggest you work with a financial professional to help you with the 401(k) transfer, or rollover, so it is done properly. It is an easy thing for a professional to do properly, but it is also an easy thing for an amateur to screw up. We do hundreds of transfers and rollovers every year.

My client Frank was going for a "Number of Jobs World Record" of some sort when I first met him at age sixty-five. After we counted all his 401(k) statements (that he could find, I am concerned there might be more out there!), it came to fourteen statements. I asked Frank how much he had saved up for retirement, and he told me about $250,000. Frank was very concerned that he did not have enough money to retire. With only $250,000 at age sixty-five and no pension, I would say Frank might be a little short. After we organized everything together and transferred the fourteen 401(k)s over to one new IRA brokerage account, I printed a statement for him and slid it across the table. The total value balance said $526,213! Frank almost fell out of his chair. Good thing I have armrests on all our office chairs.

When it comes to your retirement income, it's important to be able to pull together *all* your assets, so you can examine what you have and where, and then decide what you will do with it.

Tax-Qualified, Tax-Preferred, Tax-Deferred ... Still TAXED

Financial media often cite IRAs and 401(k)s for their tax benefits. After all, with traditional plans, you put your money in, pre-tax, and it hopefully grows for years, even decades, untaxed. That's why these accounts are called "tax-qualified" or "tax-deferred" assets. They aren't *tax-free!* Rarely does Uncle Sam allow business to continue without receiving his piece of the pie, and your retirement assets are no different. If you didn't pay taxes on the front end, you will pay taxes on the money you withdraw from these accounts in retirement. Don't get me wrong: This isn't an inherently good or bad thing; it's just the way it is. It's important to understand, though, for the sake of planning ahead.

In retirement, many people assume they will be in a lower tax bracket. Are you planning to pare down your lifestyle in retirement? Perhaps you are, and perhaps you will have substantially less income in retirement. But many of my clients tell me they want to live life more or less the same as they always have. The money they would previously have spent on business attire or gas for their commute they now want to spend on hobbies and grandchildren. That's all fine, and for many of them, it is doable, but does it put them in a lower tax bracket? Probably not.

Keep in mind, IRAs, 401(k)s, and their alternatives have a few limitations because of their special tax status. For one thing, the IRS sets limits on your contributions to these retirement accounts. If you are contributing to a 401(k) or an equivalent nonprofit or government plan, your annual contribution limit is $20,500 (as of 2022). If you are fifty or older, the IRS allows additional contributions, called "catch-up contributions," of up to $6,500 on top of the regular limit of $20,500.[45] For an IRA, the limit is $7,000, with a catch-up limit of an additional $1,000.[46]

Because their tax advantages come from their intended use as retirement income, withdrawing funds from these accounts before you turn fifty-nine-and-one-half can carry stiff penalties. In addition to fees your investment management company might charge, you will have to pay income tax *and* a 10 percent federal tax penalty, with few exceptions.

---

[45] Jackie Stewart. Kiplinger.com. December 17, 2021. "401(k) Contribution Limits for 2022." https://www.kiplinger.com/retirement/retirement-plans/401ks/603949/401k-contribution-limits-for-2022
[46] Fidelity.com. 2021."IRA contribution limits." https://www.fidelity.com/retirement-ira/contribution-limits-deadlines

The fifty-nine-and-one-half rule for retirement accounts is incredibly important to remember, especially when you're young. Younger workers are often tempted to cash out an IRA from a previous employer and then are surprised to find their checks missing 20 percent of the account value to income taxes, penalty taxes, and account fees.

Many millennials I see in my practice say, while they may be socking money away in their workplace retirement plan, it is often the *only* place they are saving. This could be problematic later because of the fifty-nine-and-one-half rule; what if you have an emergency? It is important to fund your retirement, but you need to have some liquid assets handy as emergency funds. This can help you avoid breaking into your retirement accounts and incurring taxes and penalties because of the fifty-nine-and-one-half rule.

RMDs

Remember how we talked about the 401(k) or IRA being a "tax wrapper" for your funds? Well, eventually, Uncle Sam will want a bite of that candy bar. So, when you turn seventy-two, the government requires you withdraw a portion of your account, which the IRS calculates based on the size of your account and your estimated lifespan. This required minimum distribution, or RMD, is the government's insurance it will collect some taxes, at some point, from your earnings. Because you didn't pay taxes on the front end, you will now pay income taxes on whatever you withdraw, including your RMDs. Also, let me just remind you not to play chicken with the U.S. government; if you don't take your RMDs starting at seventy-two, you will have to write a check to the IRS for *50 percent* of the amount of your missed RMDs. With the change in law from the SECURE Act of 2019, even after you begin RMDs, you can still also continue contributing to your 401(k) or IRAs if you are still employed, which can affect the whole discussion on RMDs and possible tax considerations.

If you don't need income from your retirement accounts, RMDs can seem like more of a tax burden than an income boon. While some people prefer to reinvest their RMDs, this comes with the possibility of additional taxation: You'll pay income taxes on your RMDs and then capital gains taxes on the growth of your investments. If you are legacy-minded, there are other ways to use RMDs, many of which have tax benefits.

Permanent Life Insurance
One way to turn those pesky RMDs into a legacy is through permanent life insurance. Assuming you need the death benefit coverage and can qualify for it medically, if properly structured, these products can pass on a sizeable death benefit to your beneficiaries, tax-free, as part of your general legacy plan.

ILIT
Another way to use RMDs toward your legacy is to work with an estate planning attorney to create an irrevocable life insurance trust (ILIT). This is basically a permanent life insurance policy placed within a trust. Because the trust is irrevocable, you would relinquish control of it, but, unlike with just a permanent life insurance policy, your death benefit won't count toward your taxable estate.

Annuities
Because annuities can be tax-deferred, using all or a portion of your RMDs to fund an annuity contract can be one way to further delay taxation while guaranteeing your income payments (either to you or your loved ones) later. (Assuming you don't need the RMD income during your retirement.)

Qualified Charitable Distributions
If you are charity-minded, you may use your RMDs toward a charitable organization instead of using them for income. You must do this directly from your retirement account (you can't

take the RMD check and *then* pay the charity) for your withdrawals to be qualified charitable distributions (QCDs), but this is one way of realizing some of the benefits of a charitable legacy during your own lifetime. You will not need to pay taxes on your QCDs, and they won't count toward your annual charitable tax deduction limit, plus you'll be able to see how the organization you are supporting uses your donations. You should consult a financial professional on how to correctly make a QCD, particularly since the SECURE Act has implemented a few regulations on this point.[47]

Anyone who has money in a 401(k), an IRA, a Simple or SEP IRA, a 457 plan, a 403(b), a thrift program, or any other qualified retirement program will have these forced distributions by the time they are age seventy-two. Except for one spectacular type of tax wrapper: the Roth IRA. More about my favorite type of account, the Roth IRA, in a moment.

Because of this, a client needs to have a pre-age seventy-two income plan and a post-age seventy-two income plan. Before the year you turn age seventy-two, you have the luxury of taking income from wherever you see fit. Take it from your IRA or 401(k), or don't. Whatever you want. But from age seventy-two on, you lose that control. You are forced to take taxable distributions out of your qualified retirement accounts whether you like it or not. In many cases, we find that the forced distribution a client must take is significantly higher than the income they desire for their lifestyle. This results in additional taxation on distributions that you don't want. You can almost hear Uncle Sam say, "Gotcha!"

We advocate that a client gets real clarity about the lifestyle income they want and that they project how much of that income needed is going to be covered by the required minimum distribution. This can be illustrated with any good retirement

---

[47] Bob Carlson. Forbes. January 28, 2020. "More Questions And Answers About The SECURE Act."
https://www.forbes.com/sites/bobcarlson/2020/01/28/more-questions-and-answers-about-the-secure-act/#113d49564869

income and tax planning software, like our Retirement Blueprint. Any overage needs tax planning FIRST before any other tax planning. This is just one of the reasons why time is so important in your Retirement Blueprint. If you retire at sixty-two, you have ten years to deal with this issue and prepare for your seventy-second birthday. If you retire at age sixty-five, you only have seven years. This can also have a ripple effect on your Social Security choices. Maybe even your pension choices. If you decide to enact some kind of multi-year tax plan to prepare for your age seventy-two required minimum distributions, it could have an impact on whether you decide to start guaranteed income payments sooner or later.

Roth IRA

Since the Taxpayer Relief Act of 1997, there has been a different kind of retirement account, or "tax wrapper," available to the public: the Roth. Roth IRAs and Roth 401(k)s each differ from their traditional counterparts in one big way: You pay your taxes on the front end. This means, once your post-tax money is in the Roth account, as long as you follow the rules and limitations of that account, your distributions are truly tax-free. You won't pay income tax when you take withdrawals, so, in turn, you don't have to worry about RMDs. However, Roth accounts have the same limitations as traditional 401(k)s and IRAs when it comes to withdrawing money before age fifty-nine-and-one-half, with the added stipulation that the account must have been open for at least five years in order for the account holder to make withdrawals.

If there were top awards given out to people for great retirement income and tax planning, I think the biggest qualification should be how much you have in Roth IRAs at the end. It's income-tax-free money for you and your loved ones! Having a plan to get as much into a Roth IRA as makes sense is probably the most important piece of a great retirement income and tax plan (outside of not running out of money). There is much misunderstanding about how Roths work and how to get money into them. I will say they get great press, though. Whoever is running the public relations department for Roth IRAs is doing a fantastic job. You never hear anything bad about them.

When you save money into a Roth IRA or Roth 401(k) instead of the opposite, you are giving up the year one tax deduction. That means you had to pay taxes on the money that you put into the Roth as opposed to sticking it in a traditional IRA or 401(k) and getting a tax break on day one. For clients who have a ton of responsibilities at home like little kids and a mortgage, things might be financially tight. Having that tax deduction could make a huge difference in terms of cash flow. For instance, if you save $20,000 of your income into a traditional 401(k) and you were in the 25 percent tax bracket, that deduction would save you $5,000 in taxes. That's a real $5,000 that you would get back in cash from the IRS and could use to pay your bills. I do not think it is appropriate to just say that everyone should save in the after-tax Roth 401(k) or IRA because "taxes are going to be higher down the road." It could be that your individual tax situation is just the opposite. Higher taxes now and lower down the road. (The way to discover the probability of this would be to do planning like the Retirement Blueprint, by the way).

Roth IRAs also get the awesome tag: tax-free. All the gains and contributions in a Roth IRA or 401(k) are 100 percent income-tax-free to the owner and whomever the owner names as beneficiary. This is why there are no RMDs on Roth IRAs. The government could care less if you ever take money out because there are no taxes on it. But I don't know if that tag "tax-free" is a valid description. In reality, the contributions you put into the Roth have already been taxed. Of course, you're not going to pay tax on those contributions—the principal of your Roth IRA. You already have. This is also the reason that you can withdraw that principal out of a Roth IRA with no penalty or age requirement. The government doesn't care because you've already paid tax on it and there's nothing in it for them.[48] So in reality, the Roth IRA is "partially tax-free." If you had a Roth IRA and a traditional IRA invested in the exact same stock starting at the exact same time, it would probably take a few years of earnings to break even (in favor of the traditional deductible IRA) because of the taxes you had to pay at the beginning of the Roth contribution.

Beyond that, Roth IRAs are also part of a taxpayer's estate, and although they are income-tax-free, they are not estate-tax-free. As of this writing, if you have a combined total estate value of $12.06 million or greater, you have an estate tax problem, and any Roth IRA balance would be part of this total estate value.[49] They are "partially tax-free."

This makes me sound like I don't like Roths. Absolutely not! I love them! But I want to be realistic about them. Just like many other tax strategies, Roth IRA contributions should be thought out. If you're adding money to a Roth without a little foresight, you might be missing out on valuable deductions that you really needed at critical points in your life. On the other hand, if you're completely ignoring the looming tax increases of the future and just contribute everything to the traditional deductible 401(k) or IRA to boost up your refund from the IRS, you might be setting yourself up for tax Armageddon.

What if you are at a point in life when hiring an advisor and paying a planning fee for advice on this is just not a planned expense? I have some suggestions for younger people without a written retirement income and tax plan when it comes to traditional 401(k) vs. Roth 401(k). If you are at a point in life where you have very little responsibilities and not too high of an income, saving as much on the Roth 401(k) side makes the most sense. If you are saving Roth early in the working years, that

---

[48]Amy Fontinelle. Investopedia. March 18, 2022. "How To Use Your Roth IRA as an Emergency Fund." https://www.investopedia.com/articles/personal-finance/040714/how-use-your-roth-ira-emergency-fund.asp
[49]Rocky Mengle. Kiplinger. November 10, 2021. "Estate Tax Exemption Amount Goes Up for 2022."
https://www.kiplinger.com/taxes/601639/estate-tax-exemption-2022

means that money can compound and grow in a super tax-advantaged Roth format for the longest period of time. That is what I call a "Winner Winner Chicken Dinner." The deduction you miss out on would probably not be that significant since you were not making that much money anyway. You could tighten the belt and live with it for the long-term tax benefits of the Roth. However, as you get older and those greater responsibilities and expenses come online and your wages increase, shifting those contributions to the deductible 401(k) might make more sense, at least for a few years, to increase cash flow. Then as responsibilities decrease (mortgages get paid off, kids move out, etc.), maybe shift back to saving as much on the Roth side as possible.

Regardless of what you choose to do as far as a contribution wrapper goes over the years, you will likely end up with at least some traditional IRA or traditional taxable 401(k) money. Even if you save all on the Roth side, any contributions that your employer makes into your 401(k) would be on the traditional taxable side. Meaning you've never paid any tax on that money. It is much more realistic for a typical retiree to have most of their retirement money on the traditional 401(k) side and very little or no money on the Roth side. Don't feel bad about this! Roth IRAs have only been around since 1998, and Roth 401(k)s weren't first allowed until 2006. So, if you're retiring anytime soon, you haven't had a fair chance to put a bunch of money in Roth over these last years.

This is where Roth conversions come in. A Roth conversion is when you transfer money from an IRA account to a Roth IRA account. This could be in the form of cash being transferred, or shares of mutual funds, exchange-traded funds, stock, or bonds. The conversion can be done at any time, at any age, and with no limitations on income (at least as of this writing). You do not have to be working to do a conversion either! Meaning if you have no earned income, you can convert to your heart's desire! Any IRA custodian can easily do this for you. Most 401(k) programs will also allow you to do a transfer or convert money from your traditional 401(k) side to your Roth 401(k) side. The amount you convert is totally up to you. Go ahead and convert $100 or the maximum value of the account. In most cases, you sign just one piece of paper executing the conversion with proper instructions, and poof, the money is now transferred over to the super tax-advantaged Roth side. What's the catch? It is a taxable event. You will have to pay income taxes on the value of whatever amount you decided to convert in that tax year. This will be on top of any other regular taxable income you had from work, pension, Social Security, dividends, or anything else.

This is why, for most clients, the best Retirement Blueprint has a multi-year tax plan that continues and is adjusted all throughout retirement—especially when it comes to Roth conversions. It is very rare that I find it makes sense for a client to convert all their 401(k) or IRA to Roth IRA in one gigantic swoop. More than likely, that would bump them up into a tax bracket they would have never seen in their lifetime. It makes more sense normally to do this methodically over several years. The questions you probably ask then are, "Well, how many years? How much per year?? Equal in each year, or higher in some and lower in others???" Wow, you have a lot of good questions. The answer is: I don't know, because the answer for you is different from the answer for your best friend you work with, even if they have the exact amount of money you have and want to retire on the same day. The best answer comes by doing some forecasting and mapping out the best strategy for you with a long-term retirement income and tax plan, like a Retirement Blueprint.

That said, I do have a little saying with my clients about our ongoing multi-year tax planning: "Don't let any catastrophe go to waste." When something bad happens, there is usually some kind of tax benefit we can get out of it!

In some cases, unforeseen events in the markets might create an opportunity for our clients to do heavier tax actions than originally planned. For instance, let's say we planned for you to do a $50,000 Roth conversion of mutual fund shares every year from the beginning of retirement until you turned age seventy-two. That Roth conversion is taxable, and let's say that the $50,000 target was specifically chosen to keep you in the same marginal tax bracket. Now, let's say one of the years the market has a meltdown—it goes down 50 percent (ouch)! Your $50,000 mutual fund value just dropped to $25,000. Is it still a good idea to do the Roth conversion that year? You bet! Converting the same $50,000 worth of shares may have the effect of converting $100,000 of value, assuming the market was to come back at some point. Let's say that happened. You converted $50,000 of shares in a market that was down 50 percent, and by the end of the same year, the market had recovered, and your $50,000 worth of shares rebounded to $100,000. What is the 1099-R dollar number from the Roth conversion that you are going to have to put on your tax return for that year, $50,000 or $100,000? $50,000—even though the value today has rebounded to $100,000 tax-free in the Roth! In fact, in this situation, I may suggest that you do a higher-than-average Roth conversion if it made sense. Instead of converting just $50,000, go heavy and convert $100,000 worth of shares that may act like $200,000 worth of future value!

Another awful event that could create tax opportunity is unforeseen medical or dental expenses. When this happens, it is usually big dollar numbers. Those medical expenses are partially deductible on your tax return and could result in another opportunity to do a heavy Roth conversion. For instance, let's say that you had medical expenses in a given year that gave you a "Schedule A" itemized tax deduction of $30,000 on top of your regular standard deduction from previous years. That $30,000 medical expense deduction write-off could counter a taxable $30,000 Roth conversion.

Please note that Roth conversions must be completed by December 31 of each tax year. This is very different than Roth contributions or putting new dollars in from your work earnings. Those can be added to your Roth all the way up to April 15 of the following tax year. Conversions are not new dollars. They are old dollars being moved from one account to another. This means that Roth conversions need to be planned out ahead of time, no later than early December of the current tax year.

Taking Charge

As mentioned earlier, the 401(k) and IRA have largely replaced pensions, but they aren't an equal trade.

Pensions are employer-funded; the money feeding into them is money that wouldn't ever show up on your pay stub. Because 401(k)s are self-funded, you must actively and consciously save. This distinction has made a difference when it comes to funding retirement. The average 401(k) balance for a person age sixty to sixty-nine is $195,500, but the median likely tells the full story. The median 401(k) balance for a person age sixty to sixty-nine is $62,000. A general suggestion derived from those statistics is to aim, by age thirty, to have saved an amount equal to 50 to 100 percent of your annual salary.[50] For some thirty-year-olds, saving half an annual salary by age thirty is more than some sixty-to-sixty-nine-year-olds have saved for their entire lives.

There can be many reasons why people underfund their retirement plans, like being overwhelmed by the investment choices or taking withdrawals from IRAs when they leave an employer. Still, the reason at the top of the list is this: People simply aren't participating to begin with.

So, whether you use a 401(k) with an employer or an IRA alternative with a private company, separate from your workplace, the most important retirement savings decision you can make is to sock away your money somewhere in the first place.

---

[50] Arielle O'Shea. Nerd Wallet. March 17, 2021. "The Average 401(k) Balance by Age." https://www.nerdwallet.com/article/investing/the-average-401k-balance-by-age

CHAPTER 7

Annuities

In my practice, I offer my clients a variety of products—from securities to insurance—all designed to help them reach their financial goals. You may be wondering: Why single out a single product in this book?

Well, while most of my clients have a pretty good understanding of business and finance, I sometimes find those who have the impression there must be magic involved. Some people assume there is a magic finance wand we can wave to change years' worth of savings into a strategy for retirement income. But it's not as easy as a goose laying golden eggs or the Fairy Godmother turning a pumpkin into a coach!

Finances aren't magic; it takes lots of hard work and, typically, several financial products and strategies to pull together a complete retirement plan. Of all the financial products I work with, it seems people find none more mysterious than annuities. And, if I may say, even some of those who recognize the word "annuity" have a limited understanding of the product. So, in the interest of demystifying annuities, let me tell you a little about what an annuity is.

In general, insurance is a financial hedge against risk. Car owners buy auto insurance to protect their finances in case they injure someone or someone injures them. Homeowners have house insurance to protect their finances in case of a fire, flood, or another disaster. People have life insurance to protect their finances in case of untimely death. Almost juxtaposed to life insurance, people have annuities in case of a long life; annuities can give you financial protection by providing consistent and reliable income payments.

The basic premise of an annuity is you, the annuitant, pay an insurance company some amount in exchange for their contractual guarantee they will pay you income for a certain time period. How that company pays you, for how long, and how much they offer are all determined by the annuity contract you enter into with the insurance company.

How You Get Paid

There are two ways for an annuity contract to provide income: The first is through what is called annuitization, and the second is through the use of income riders. We'll get into income riders in a bit, but let's talk about annuitization. That nice, long word is, in my opinion, one reason annuities have a reputation for mystery and misinformation.

Annuitization

When someone "annuitizes" a contract, it is the point where he or she turns on the income stream. Once a contract has been annuitized, there is no going back. With annuities, if the policyholder lives longer than the insurance company planned, the insurance company is still obligated to pay him or her, even if the payments end up being way more than the contract's actual value. If, however, the policyholder dies an untimely death, depending on the contract type, the insurance company may keep anything left of the money that funded the annuity—nothing would be paid out to the contract holder's survivors. You see where that could make some people balk? Now, modern annuities rarely rely on annuitization for the income portion of the contract, and instead have so many bells and whistles that the old concept of annuitization seems outdated, but because this is still an option, it's important to at least understand the basic concept.

Riders

Speaking of bells and whistles, let's talk about riders. Modern annuities have a lot of different options these days, many in the form of riders you can add to your contract for a fee—usually about 1 percent of the contract value per year. Each rider has its particulars, and the types of riders available will vary by the type of annuity contract purchased, but I'll just briefly outline some of these little extras:

- Lifetime income rider: Contract guarantees you an enhanced income for life
- Death benefit rider: Contract pays an enhanced death benefit to your beneficiaries even if you have annuitized
- Return of premium rider: Guarantees you (or your beneficiaries) will at least receive back the premium value of the annuity
- Long-term care rider: Provides a certain amount, sometimes as much as twice the principal value of the contract, to help pay for long-term care if the contract holder is moved to a nursing home or assisted living situation

This isn't an extensive look, and usually the riders have fancier names based on the issuing company, like "Lorem Ipsum Insurance Company Income Preferred Bonus Fixed Index Annuity rider," but I just wanted to show you what some of the general options are in layperson's terms.

Types of Annuities

Annuities break down into four basic types: immediate, variable, fixed, and fixed index.

Immediate

Immediate annuities primarily rely on annuitization to provide income—you give the insurance company a lump sum up front, and your payments begin immediately. Once you begin receiving income payments, the transaction is irreversible, and you no longer have access to your money in a lump sum. When you die, any remaining contract value is typically forfeited to the insurance company.

All other annuity contract types are "deferred" contracts, meaning you fund your policy as a lump sum or over a period of years and you give it the opportunity to grow over time—sometimes years, sometimes decades.

Variable

A variable annuity is an insurance contract as well as an investment. It's sold by insurance companies, but only through someone who is registered to sell investment products. With a variable annuity contract, the insurance company invests your premiums in subaccounts that are tied to the stock market. This makes it a bit different from the other annuity contract types because it is the only contract where your money is subject to losses because of market declines. Your contract value has a greater opportunity to grow, but it also stands to lose. Additionally, your contract's value will be subject to the underlying investment's fees and limitations—including capital gains taxes, management fees, etc. Once it is time for you to receive income from the contract, the insurance company will pay you a certain income, locked in at whatever your contract's value was.

There are two main reasons I see clients use a variable annuity. One I like, and the other I do not like so much.

The first reason, and the one I like, is to have market-based investments with tax deferral. Variable annuities enable clients to avoid current taxation with some of their non-qualified or non-IRA-type money. Any gains in the account are deferred from taxes until withdrawn by the owner. This goes for any internal interest or dividends creating a change in the subaccount unit value inside the variable annuity. The owner can change investment subaccounts with no capital gain or income tax event. Clients can manage investment choices on their own, like a self-invested brokerage account. They can also hire a professional money manager to manage the variable annuity for them.

However, this tax deferral comes at a price. On top of the normal internal subaccount management fees that go to the investment houses available inside the variable annuity, the insurance company offering the variable annuity charges their own separate fee. It is called a mortality and expense risk fee, or M&E fee. That fee can vary, but we find it averages around -1.5 percent industry-wide. Add the M&E fee to an average investment house internal fee of -1 percent and you have a total average fee of about -2.5 percent. That is pretty expensive.

To put that in perspective, on a $100,000 variable annuity account with a 2.5 percent fee, that comes to $2,500 per year. That's a real $2,500 that works against your account value regardless of whether it makes money. So just a break-even on the fees your subaccounts must earn $2,500; if your subaccount earns 0 percent, you are going to see your value drop by $2,500. If the variable annuity you happen to be in has an internal combined fee of -3.5 percent, that's $3,500 in the same example! Because of this, I feel variable annuities make more sense for high-income earners that are trying to avoid high-income taxation on unused assets, and an analysis should be done on the probable annual taxes of a non-qualified brokerage account vs.

the annual fees being paid inside the variable annuity by the client.

Also, let's just be clear on what tax-deferred means: the taxation on the gains is pushed down the road to a later date. The taxes due are not canceled. It is tax deferral, not tax avoidance. Someone is going to eventually pay the taxes on any gains. Maybe it's you, maybe it's your kids, maybe it's some other beneficiary. The deferred tax problem would need to be analyzed and weighed against the massive stepped-up cost basis tax break your family would receive if invested in non-qualified equities at your death.

The other reason I see people buy a variable annuity, and the one I don't like so much, is to have a guaranteed income source. All the fees I wrote about above are still included in this type of variable annuity setup, but on top of them, the owner purchases an extra benefit for guaranteed income. This comes in the form of a rider added to the variable annuity that will guarantee lifetime income for the owner. The owner has an additional fee, and the average industry-wide is about -1 percent. Now, I am not anti-guaranteed income. If anything, I am very pro-guaranteed income. But I am anti-guaranteed income if it's going to cost 3.5 percent per year in fees for my client! Especially when there are alternative annuity options that guarantee income the exact same way with no fee.

Fixed

A traditional fixed annuity is pretty straightforward. You purchase a contract with a guaranteed interest rate and, when you are ready, the insurance company will make regular income payments to you at whatever payout rate your contract guarantees. Those payments will continue for the rest of your life and, if you choose, for the remainder of your spouse's life.

Fixed annuities don't have much in the way of upside potential, but many people like them for their guarantees (after all, if your Aunt May lives to be ninety-five, knowing she has a paycheck later in life can be her mental and financial safety net), as well as for their predictability. Unlike variable annuities, which are subject to market risk and might be up one year and down the next, you can easily calculate the value of your fixed annuity over your lifetime.

Fixed Index

To recap, variable annuities take on more risk to offer more possibilities to grow. Fixed annuities have less potential growth, but they protect your principal. In the last couple of decades, many insurance companies have retooled their product line to offer fixed index annuities, which are sort of midway between variable and fixed annuities on that risk/reward spectrum. Fixed index annuities offer greater growth potential than traditional fixed annuities but less than variable annuities. Like traditional fixed annuities, however, fixed index annuities are protected from downside market losses.

Fixed index annuities earn interest that is tied to the market, meaning that, instead of your contract value growing at a set interest rate like a traditional fixed annuity, it has the potential to grow within a range. Your contract's value is credited interest based on the performance of an external market index like the S&P 500 while never being invested in the market itself. You can't invest in the S&P 500 directly, but each year, your annuity as the potential to earn interest based on the chosen index's performance, submit to limits set by the company such as caps, spreads and participation rates. For instance, if your contract caps your interest at 5 percent, then in a year that the S&P 500 gains 3 percent, your annuity value increases 3 percent. If the S&P 500 gains 35 percent, your annuity value gets a 5 percent interest bump. But since your money isn't actually invested in the market with a fixed index annuity, if the market nosedives (such as happened during 2000, 2008 and 2020, anyone?) you won't see any increase in your contract value. Conversely, there will also be no decrease in your contract value—no matter how badly the market performed, as long as you follow the terms of the contract, you won't lose any of the interest you were credited in previous years.

So, what if the S&P 500 shows a market loss of 30 percent? Your contract value isn't going anywhere (unless you purchased an optional rider—this charge will still come out of your annuity value each year). For those who are more interested in protection than growth potential, fixed index annuities can be an attractive option because, when the stock market has a long period of positive performance, a fixed index annuity can enjoy conservative growth. And, during stretches where the stock market is erratic and stock values across the board take significant losses? Fixed index annuities won't lose anything due to the stock market volatility.

There are a couple of ways that I see our clients use fixed index annuities. The first is as an ultra-conservative accumulation vehicle. I believe that a good one should give a client about a +4 percent per year average rate of return, and a great one closer to +5 percent per year average. That is a tremendous rate of return clients would have received compared to bank CDs during this ultra-low interest rate environment. You would've been lucky to get an average of +2 percent in a CD over the past decade. There are no fees or charges inside a fixed index annuity (assuming you don't have any riders attached), so that means you earn the entire return. If you earn 5 percent, you get the whole 5 percent. Add the tax deferral benefit of the annuity and now you need a 6 percent rate to return in the non-qualified CD to break even, assuming you were in the 20 percent tax bracket on that CD interest.

The second way I see clients use a fixed index annuity is to provide guaranteed income. All the top insurance companies out there today offer some kind of product that has a guaranteed lifetime income rider available for a fee, or a benefit built right into the product for free. What a lifetime income benefit does is guarantees an income to the owner for the rest of their life, even if after taking out money for many years the annuity finally runs out of money. The best of those products will continue guaranteed lifetime income to a surviving spouse as well.

This is not a magic well. You are probably asking yourself: "How can the insurance company afford to do that?" Well, they are not giving you any of their money first. You're using your own money first for those guaranteed lifetime income withdrawals. It's only if you completely run your account value down to zero that the insurance company must pay any benefits out of their own pockets. Also, the guaranteed income payment is determined by the company. These payment agreements vary from product to product, and you want to understand them thoroughly before you purchase. In a nutshell, what you are doing if you are considering a fixed index annuity with a lifetime income benefit is constructing your own private pension.

Now, all of this safety, good rates of return, and guaranteed income sounds great, doesn't it? What's the catch? Well, of course, you knew that was coming. The catch is the time commitment on the money. Any fixed annuity you consider is going to have some kind of time commitment. Most of the quality products we see that offer guaranteed lifetime income benefits are a ten-year time commitment. However, if you are just looking for accumulation only (no guaranteed lifetime income benefit), you can go as short as five years. These are called the surrender charge periods, and the surrender charges are very high if you decide to completely cancel the annuity before the time period is up. Most quality annuity products offer a certain amount the client can withdraw every year without penalty before the surrender period is completed. I find that is usually 10 percent per year. In that case, if you had $100,000 in a fixed index annuity, you would be able to take out $10,000 per year, every year, with no penalty whatsoever. If you took out $15,000 instead, you would get the $10,000 penalty-free, but the additional $5,000 would have a surrender charge assessed on it. Of course, this has nothing to do with taxes that might be due. A lot of companies also offer emergency provisions that lift all surrender charges if the reason someone needs access is because of medical incapacitation or terminal illness. The best also have no surrender charges to beneficiaries if the owner were to die before the surrender period is completed. Once you have completed the surrender charge period, insurance companies do not kick you out or make you start over. After that, you can keep your money in the annuity as long as you want, completely liquid.

Here is what I will say about safety, liquidity (meaning how much of your money can you access with no penalty), and getting a good rate of return. You can never get all three. The best you can ever get is two out of the three. Name any investment—any. It will only have two of these three traits. It could be safe and liquid, like a savings account, but with a low rate of return. Or it could be liquid and have the potential for a good return, like a stock, but not safe. Or it could be safe with the potential for a good return like a long-term CD, bond, or fixed index annuity, but it will come with the time commitment. Anything that is truly safe and secure and has the potential for decent return is going to come with a time commitment. That's the trade-off—always.

I would suggest you work with an insurance broker that offers multiple companies to choose from. If you're shooting for accumulation, ask what the top two or three accumulation products are that they offer. If you're shooting for guaranteed income, what are the two guaranteed income fixed index annuities? My firm has contracts with over thirty carriers. All of them have unique products that make a lot of sense for some clients, but not others. Any decision you make on this should be very specific to your goals and purpose and made without serious forethought on what you're trying to achieve.

Other Things to Know About Annuities

We just talked about the four kinds of annuity contracts available, but all of them have some commonalities as annuities.

For all annuities, the contractual guarantees are only as strong as the insurance company that sells the product, which makes it important to thoroughly check the credit ratings of any company whose products you are considering.

Annuities are tax-deferred, meaning you don't have to pay taxes on interest earnings each year as the contract value grows. Instead, you will pay ordinary income taxes on your withdrawals. These are meant to be long-term products, so, like other tax-deferred or tax-advantaged products, if you begin taking withdrawals from your contract before age fifty-nine-and-one-half, you may also have to pay a 10 percent federal tax penalty. Also, while annuities are generally considered illiquid, most contracts allow you to withdraw up to 10 percent of your contract value every year. Withdraw any more, however, and you could incur additional surrender penalties.

Keep in mind, your withdrawals will deplete the accumulated cash value, death benefit, and, possibly, the rider values of your contract.

I believe that all financial products available to the public and regulated by the government should be considered as possible tools to achieve a client's retirement goals. I do not understand why some financial advisors have a financial product bias and choose to ignore certain tools just because of what they are called.

Could you imagine if you were working with a home builder, and he had a bias against screwdrivers? What if you found out later that he smashed all the screws of your new house in with hammers when they could have been screwed in properly with a screwdriver, just because he refused to learn how the screwdriver worked? Does that make any sense?

If you're working with a financial professional who only offers security products and does not offer any insurance or annuity products, you are working with a contractor like that. On the flip side, if you're working with an insurance salesperson that does not offer any security products, you are also working with a biased advisor. Most of our clients need security market-based products to achieve their long-term growth goals combined with the safety of annuity products to give them the guaranteed income they need in retirement. Every client is different. Some clients might end up needing everything in stocks and bonds, others might need everything safe and secure in CDs and fixed annuities. But most hard-working Americans need that balance to give them a sense of security for income over the retirement years and still know that their money can grow long-term.

So, what determines whether an annuity makes sense for you? Annuities are just another financial tool you may or may not use to build your financial house. I would suggest first to get clarity on exactly what it is you wanted your money to do for you over your retirement years, and then consider recommendations to help achieve those goals. We call that a Retirement Blueprint around our office.

What is the absolute number one fear of the typical American about to retire? Running out of money in retirement. The reality is that we are all living longer, healthier lives. But this longevity has created another problem: outliving our money. As I wrote about earlier, our grandparents' generation had guaranteed monthly pension payments, many of them with annual cost-of-living increases over the years. Many of my new clients want something similar and hire me to engineer their own private pension for them.

This is where my industry has really fallen short. Most of the education that is provided to the public on income planning all surrounds dividends on stock, ETFs, or mutual funds. So, for example, let's pretend you retire with $5 million combined in your 401(k), IRAs, and brokerage accounts. You hire an investment professional, and they help you to build a portfolio getting a 3 percent dividend yield on investments inside. That would be $150,000 you could live on every year, just in dividend payments. That on top of your Social Security would probably be a comfortable retirement for most Americans. Let's change the dollar number a bit now. Instead of having $5 million saved up for yourself, let's say you have a grand total of $500,000. That $500,000 at the same 3 percent dividend yield would only be $15,000 per year income. That combined with your Social Security would equal ... maybe you're gonna run out of money.

The problem here is that many people in my industry approach the $5 million client the same way they approach the $500,000 client. They are offering both of those clients the same financial medicine—the same 100 percent security-based portfolios to try to achieve their goals. The reality is they are two very different households and need very different suggestions. One of the beautiful things we have found by using a fixed index annuity with a guaranteed lifetime income benefit built-in is that it can give that guaranteed pension-like income for assets dedicated to the Income Bucket and still allow for a good amount of assets to grow long-term in the Growth Bucket, probably in the stock market. The client might end up running the Income Bucket completely out of money in the annuity. Actually, this is a good thing if that's what the client was trying to achieve!

Let's say fifteen years into a retirement income plan the client has run their fixed index annuity down to zero from lifetime income payments, but they still have a guarantee of $50,000 per year for life from the insurance company, on top of their Social Security. They just shifted the responsibility of creating retirement income over to a giant insurance company! The client does not have to deal with it anymore. Plus, they still have a bunch of money in their Growth Bucket.

Annuities aren't for everyone, but it's important to understand them before saying "yea" or "nay" on whether they fit into your plan; otherwise, you're not operating with complete information, wouldn't you agree? Regardless, you should talk to a financial professional who can help you understand annuities, help you dissect your particular financial needs, and help show you whether an annuity is appropriate for your retirement income plan.

CHAPTER 8

Estate & Legacy

I n my practice, I devote a significant portion of my time to matters of estates. That doesn't mean drawing up wills or trusts or putting together powers of attorney or anything like that. After all, I'm not an estate planning attorney. But I am a financial professional, and what part of the "estate" isn't affected by money matters?

I've included this chapter because I have seen many people do estate planning wrong. Clients, or clients' families, have come in after experiencing a death in the family and have found themselves in the middle of probate, high taxes, or a discovery of something unforeseen (often long-term care) draining the estate.

I have also seen people do estate planning right: clients or families who visit my office to talk about legacies and how to make them last and adult children who have room to grieve without an added burden of unintended costs, without stress from a family ruptured because of inadequate planning.

I'll share some of these stories here. However, I'm not going to give you specific advice, since everyone's situation is unique. I only want to give you some things to think about and to underscore the importance of planning ahead.

My first attorney relationship and my most personal was with my dad, Edward F. Downey, Sr., Attorney at Law. Dad referred me to many of my first clients, and a few of them we still serve today! As of this writing, Dad is ninety-one years old and no longer practicing law. In addition to the few who are still with us, I have many clients who are children of those original clients from the 1990s.

Between Dad, the attorney, and my Uncle Marty, the CPA, I learned early in my career that helping clients with retirement income, investment, tax, and estate planning was a multi-faceted process that needed multiple professionals helping each household, with each planning specialty being just as important as the other. I guess you can say I was kind of baptized into financial planning in this manner. Today, we have multiple relationships with CPAs and attorneys. In many cases, one type of attorney will specialize in a specific type of law, but not another. For instance, we have one attorney who specializes in Medicaid estate planning, another who focuses on family estate planning, and another for special needs beneficiary planning. A good financial advisor needs multiple relationships to help with clients' specific needs.

You Can't Take It With You

When it comes to legacy and estate planning, the most important thing is to *do it*. I have heard people from clients to celebrities (rap artist Snoop Dogg comes to mind) say they aren't interested in what happens to their assets when they die because they'll be dead. That's certainly one way to look at it. But I think that's a very selfish way to go about things—we all have people and causes we care about, and those who care about us. Even if the people we love don't *need* what we leave behind, they can still be fined or legally tied up in the probate process or burial costs if we don't plan for those. And that's not even considering what happens if you become incapacitated at some point while you are still alive. Having a plan in place can greatly reduce the stress of those responsibilities on your loved ones; it's just a loving thing to do.

Documents

There are a few documents that lay the groundwork of legacy planning. You've probably heard of all or most of them, but I'd like to review what they are and how people commonly use them. These are all things you should talk about with an estate planning attorney to establish your legacy.

Powers of Attorney

A power of attorney, or POA, is a document giving someone the authority to act on your behalf and in your best interests. These come in handy in situations where you cannot be present (think a vacation where you get stuck in Canada) or, for durable powers of attorney, even when you are incapacitated (think in a coma or coping with dementia).

It is important to have powers of attorney in place and to appoint someone you trust to act on your behalf in these matters. Have you ever heard of someone who was incapacitated after a car accident, whether from head trauma or being in a coma for weeks—sometimes months? Do you think their bills stopped coming due during that time? I like my phone company and my bank, but neither one is about to put a moratorium on sending me bills, particularly not for an extended or interminable period. A power of attorney would have the authority to pay your mortgage or cancel your cable while you are unable.

You can have multiple POAs
and require them to act jointly.
What this looks like: Do you think two heads are better than one? One man, Chris, significantly relied on his two sons' opinions for both his business and personal matters. He appointed both sons as joint POA, requiring both their signoffs for his medical and financial matters.

*You can have multiple POAs
who can act independently.*

What this looks like: Irene had three children with whom she routinely stayed. They lived in different areas of the country, which she thought was an advantage; one month she might be hiking out West, the next she could enjoy the newest off-Broadway production, and the next she could soak up some Southern sun. She named her three children as independently authorized POAs, so, if something happened, no matter where she was, the child closest could step in to act on her behalf.

*You can have POAs who have
different responsibilities.*

What this looks like: Although Luke's friend Claire, a nurse, was his go-to and POA for health-related issues, financial matters usually made her nervous, so he appointed his good neighbor, Matt, as his POA in all of his financial and legal matters.

In addition to POAs, it may be helpful to have an advanced medical directive. This is a document where you have pre-decided what choices you would make about different health scenarios. An advanced medical directive can help ease the burden for your medical POA and loved ones, particularly when it comes to end-of-life care.

Wills

Perhaps the most basic document of legacy planning, a will is a legal document wherein you outline your wishes for your estate. When it comes to your estate after your death, having a will is the foundation of your legacy. Without one, your loved ones are left behind, guessing what you would have wanted, and the court will likely split your assets according to the state's defaults. Maybe that's exactly what you wanted, as far as anyone knows, right? Because even if you told your nephew he could have your car he's been driving, if it's not in writing, it still might go to the brother, sister, son, or daughter to whom you aren't speaking.

However, it may not be enough just to have a will. Even with a will, your assets will be subject to probate. Probate is what we call the state's process for determining a will's validity. A judge will go through your will to question if it conflicts with state law, if it is the most up-to-date document, if you were mentally competent at the time it was in order, etc. For some, this is a quick, easily-resolved process. For others, particularly if someone steps forward to contest the will, it may take years to settle, all the while subjecting the assets to court costs and attorney's fees.

One other undesirable piece of the probate process is that it is a public process. That means anyone can go to the courthouse, ask for copies of the case, and discover your assets. They can also see who is slated to receive what and who is disputing.

We had a client whose best friend named him as one of the beneficiaries of his estate (he was not a client of ours and I never met him). The friend had no children and was never married, and his only sibling had died years earlier. The friend was very successful in his career as a public school administrator. When he retired, he had properties in Illinois, Michigan, and Florida, as well as $2 million in brokerage account investments. Unfortunately, he had a very simple will and there was no power of attorney included.

The first tragic thing that occurred was the friend being diagnosed with Alzheimer's disease just five years into his retirement at age sixty-five. Within thirty-six months, he was completely incapacitated. My client—his best friend and the closest thing to a living family member—stepped in to help with day-to-day activities as much as possible. But because there was no power of attorney, my client had no authority to help his friend in any legal capacity. Part of the crazy probate process on the friend's estate actually started before he died in order for someone to take charge of the friend's finances. A judge in a courtroom had to make that decision for the friend, as he was no longer able to make his own decisions. It was at that point that my client tried to get us involved to see if we could help. But the die had been cast at that point. No significant legal documents beyond the simple will had been set up by the friend, and he had no direct heirs. This was going to be extremely difficult for any private attorney to unwind.

Tragically, the Illinois court decided that the state of Illinois would be best served to help the friend, and he became a ward of the state of Illinois. That meant that a court-appointed custodian (a state government employee) had full control of all medical, residential, and financial decisions.

The friend remained a ward of the state of Illinois for the rest of his life. He was bounced around from one Illinois nursing home to another until his death six years later.

After his death, my client hired his own attorney to start the probate process to get the inheritance from the friend's estate. It was my client's belief that the estate was worth at least $3 million. He was right. However, it took five more years for us to confirm that. That's how long the probate process took after the friend's death for the state of Illinois to determine that my client was an actual beneficiary. He received 50 percent of the estate value six years after the death of the friend. But when he got the check, he was shocked. Of the $1.5 million settlement, he received $1.4 million. $100,000 went toward legal fees between the state of Illinois and my client's attorney, right? No! It was $200,000 in legal fees because there were two beneficiaries. The legal fees were the same for each!

It's also important to remember beneficiary lines trump wills. So, that large life insurance policy? What if, when you bought it fifteen years ago, you wrote your ex-husband's name on the beneficiary line? Even if you stipulate otherwise in your will, the company that holds your policy will pay out to your ex-spouse. Or, how about the thousands of dollars in your IRA you dedicated to the children thirty years ago, but one of your children was killed in a car accident, leaving his wife and two toddlers behind? That IRA is going to transfer to your remaining children, with nothing for your daughter-in-law and grandchildren.

That may paint a grim portrait, but I can't underscore enough the importance of working with a skilled estate planning attorney to keep your will and beneficiary lines up to date as your life changes.

The most horrific estate planning story that comes to my mind has to be Aretha Franklin's. I loved Aretha Franklin. I first saw her in one of my favorite movies: *The Blues Brothers*. She was for sure a no-nonsense lady. She was notorious for demanding to be paid in cash anywhere she performed—before she would set foot on stage. I guess getting taken advantage of early in her career taught her some valuable lessons. Aretha had a very weak estate plan, though. Her estate is estimated to be worth over $80 million, and even though she passed away in 2018, it still seems to be deep in the probate process, with no signs of settlement anytime soon.

I don't think Aretha had the easiest life. She had to fight hard for everything she earned. I am sure there were people in her life she absolutely did not want to get any of her money, but I'm also sure there are loved ones and charities she strongly hoped would benefit from her estate. On top of that, I think Aretha would be rolling in her grave if she understood the amount of money that has already been spent on attorneys to get this thing taken care of for her. I believe this stituation could have been settled if Aretha would've had a trust set up for her estate.

Trusts

Another piece of legacy planning to consider is the trust.

A trust is set up through an attorney and allows a third party, or trustee, to hold your assets and determine how they will pass to your beneficiaries. Many people are skeptical of trusts because they assume trusts are only appropriate for the fabulously wealthy.

However, a simple trust will likely cost more than $1,000 if prepared by an attorney and fees can be higher for couples.[51] But a trust can help you avoid both the expense and publicity of probate, provide a more immediate transfer of wealth, avoid some taxes, and provide you greater control over your legacy.

For instance, if you want to set aside some funds for a grandchild's college education, you can make it a requirement he or she enrolls in classes before your trust will dispense any funds. Like a will, beneficiary lines will override your trust conditions, so you must still keep insurance policies and other assets up to date.

Like any financial or legal consideration, there are many options these days beyond the simple "yes or no" question of whether to have a trust. For one thing, you will need to consider if you want your trust to be revocable (you can change the terms while you are alive) or irrevocable (can't be changed; you are no longer the "owner" of the contents). A brief note here about irrevocable trusts: Although they have significant and greater tax benefits, they are still subject to a Medicaid look-back period. This means, if you transfer your assets into an irrevocable trust in an attempt to shelter them from a Medicaid spend-down, you will be ineligible for Medicaid coverage of long-term care for five years. Yet, an irrevocable trust can avoid both probate and estate taxes, and it can even protect assets from legal judgments against you.

Another thing to remember when it comes to trusts, in general, is, even if you have set up a trust, you must remember to fund it. In my years of work, I've had numerous clients come to me, assuming they have protected their assets with a trust. When we talk about taxes and other pieces of their legacy, it turns out they never retitled any assets or changed any paperwork on the assets they wanted in the trust. So, please remember, a trust is just a

---

[51] Rickie Houston. smartasset.com. "How Much Does It Cost to Set Up a Trust?" https://smartasset.com/estate-planning/how-much-does-it-cost-to-set-up-a-trust

bunch of fancy legal papers if you haven't followed through on retitling your assets.

Taxes

Although charitable contributions, trusts, and other tax-efficient strategies can reduce your tax bill, it's unlikely your estate will be passed on entirely tax-free. Yet, when it comes to building a legacy that can last for generations, taxes can be one of the heaviest drains on the impact of your hard work.

For 2020, the federal estate exemption was $11.58 million per individual and $23.16 million for a married couple, with estates facing up to a 40 percent tax rate after that. In 2022, those limits increased to $12.06 million for individuals and $24.12 million for married couples, with the 40 percent top level gift and estate tax remaining the same. Currently, the new estate limits are set to increase with inflation until January 1, 2026, when they will "sunset" back to the inflation-adjusted 2017 limits.[52] And that's not taking into account the various state regulations and taxes regarding estate and inheritance transfers.

Another tax concern "frequent flyer": retirement accounts.

Your IRA or 401(k) can be a source of tax issues when you pass away. For one thing, taking funds from a sizeable account can trigger a large tax bill. However, if you leave the assets in the account, there are still required minimum distributions (RMDs), which will take effect even after you die. If you pass the account to your spouse, he or she can keep taking your RMDs as is, or your spouse can retitle the account in his or her name and receive RMDs based on his or her life expectancy. Remember, if you don't take your RMDs, the IRS will take up to 50 percent of whatever your required distribution was, plus you will still have to pay

---

[52] Laura Sanders, Richard Rubin. The Wall Street Journal. March 10, 2022. "Estate and Gift Taxes 2021-2022: "What's New This Year and What You Need to Know." https://www.wsj.com/articles/estate-and-gift-taxes-what-to-know-2021-2022-11646426764

income taxes whenever you withdraw that money. Thanks to the enactment of the SECURE Act, anyone who inherits your IRA, with few exceptions (your spouse, a beneficiary less than ten years younger, or a disabled adult child, to name a few), will need to empty the account within ten years of your death.[53]

Also—and this is a pretty big also—check with an attorney if you are considering putting your IRA or 401(k) in a trust. An improperly titled beneficiary form for the IRA could mean the difference of thousands of dollars in taxes. This is just one more reason to work with a financial professional, one who can strategically partner with an estate planning attorney to diligently check your decisions.

Estate planning is the final step of our Retirement Blueprint process. It is the third and final phase your financial life: the distribution phase. The phase when you pass away and the money you have worked so hard to build is distributed to the people and entities you cherish.

You have worked hard to build up what you have. Maybe some of what you have was inherited from your mom and dad. How hard did they have to work? Wouldn't it make sense to have a complimentary consultation with an attorney somewhere to talk about a living will or a trust? If you decide to leave it up to chance, there's a very good probability that your money will go to the "last person in the world" you would've wanted it to. Worse than that, if you become incapacitated with no power of attorney, maybe that same person is the one who shows up to make decisions for you!

We also find that many people have a misunderstanding about estate taxes. I think a lot of people believe they don't exist anymore. They are wrong. If you have an estate over $12 million currently, you have an estate tax problem because of the federal exemption. For a lot of readers, that is a comforting number that might give you the impression that you are a long, long way from

---

[53] Julia Kagan. Investopedia. October 11, 2020. "Stretch IRA." https://www.investopedia.com/terms/s/stretch-ira.asp

any estate tax problem. It is my belief that the federal estate tax exemption number will decrease significantly, maybe down to $5 million, to get our country out of the debt hole it is in. After all, who are the easiest people to tax? Dead people! They don't vote anymore.

Where a $12 million dollar estate may seem like an unachievable value, a $5 million estate might be achieved pretty easily when you start adding in houses, 401(k)s, IRAs, brokerage accounts, life insurance, etc. Planning for possible estate taxes needs the expertise of an experienced estate planning attorney, combined with a financial advisor.

In my opinion, a Retirement Blueprint is not truly completed until this is achieved. I love it when we have a new client household that has addressed all the key phases: accumulation, income, and distribution. It's like the *Lion King* "Circle of Life," but with money! This usually takes time. We see most of our clients get their retirement income and investments items done first, then attack the taxes on the retirement income, and then last, but not least, address the estate planning issues. This is just another reason why we need to meet with our clients regularly every year.

CHAPTER 9

Indexed Universal Life Insurance

My clients are not typically gamblers. A day at the casino is more likely to give them nightmares than it is to make them eager with dollar signs in their eyes. Many would rather work with at least some guarantees than with primarily stocks and risk-based products, so, of course, that often means turning more toward life insurance, and often to a product called indexed universal life insurance, also commonly referred to as fixed indexed universal life insurance.

If you've never heard of that before, I'm not surprised. This life insurance product isn't suitable for everyone, but I want to take a second to talk about it because, for the right person, it can be a significant product in their financial arsenal.

Insurance: The Basics

If you haven't been casting around in the life insurance pond much, then let's take a second to cover the basics. During our working lives, it's likely we have some kind of basic term life policy, either privately or through our employers. Term life insurance means an individual is protected for a certain period of time—usually ten to thirty years. It typically correlates to a certain amount of wages (if it's an employer's plan) or a coverage amount chosen by the individual (if it's a person's private insurance).

At its most basic, term insurance provides funds for our loved ones and can be used for a number of purposes, including covering funeral expenses or something of that nature. Oftentimes, people will take out more than this—for instance, families with a stay-at-home parent sometimes purchase policies based on the working parent's life to cover years of income, plus the mortgage, etc. Your premium for a term life policy will be based on things like your coverage limit, your age, your health, and the term of the policy.

The older you are, the more likely it is you have health events or other issues that could make it more difficult to obtain term life insurance and the more expensive it is. Some consumers may see this as a disadvantage of term life insurance because they pay into a policy for twenty years, and then it reaches its "endowment"— the end of the contract term—and there are no additional benefits.

Permanent Insurance

Aside from the basic term life policies many wage-earners hold, insurance companies also have permanent policies, also sometimes referred to as "cash value insurance." With a permanent insurance contract, your policy will typically remain in force as long as you continue to keep it funded (there is an exception for whole life policies, which we'll get to later). A permanent insurance contract has two pieces: the death benefit and cash value accumulation.

Both are spelled out in your contract. As these products gained recognition, people began to realize the products had significant advantages when it came to taxes. I don't really want to get too technical, but it is really the technical details that make these policies valuable to their owners. That bit about tax advantages makes permanent life insurance policies attractive to consumers because, not only do they receive an income-tax-free death benefit for their beneficiaries, they may also be able to borrow against their policy, income-tax-free, if they end up needing the money.

For example, let's say Emma purchases a life insurance policy when she's thirty. She hates the idea of not having anything to show for her premiums over ten to twenty years, so she decides to use a permanent policy. Then, when she's close to fifty, her brother finds himself in dire straits. Emma wants to help, and she's been a diligent saver. The catch is most of her money is in products like her 401(k) or an annuity. These may be fabulous products suitable for her needs, but her circumstance has just changed, and she's looking for ways to help her sibling without incurring significant tax penalties.

But wait . . . she has that permanent life insurance policy! She can borrow any accumulated cash value against her policy, free of income taxes. So, let's say she borrows a few thousand dollars from her policy. She doesn't have to pay taxes on any of it. She can pay it back into her policy at any time. Then, let's say Emma dies before she "settles up" her policy (or pays back that loan). As long as she continued paying premium payments or otherwise kept her policy adequately funded until she died, then her beneficiaries will still receive a death benefit, minus the policy loan.

Are you with me so far? Here are the central themes on properly structured permanent life insurance policies: tax-free death benefit and income-tax-free withdrawals through policy loans are available as long as the premiums continue to be paid, and a minimum rate of cash value accumulation is guaranteed by the strength of the insurer.

Now, let's dive a little deeper into the two basic categories of permanent insurance on the market: whole life policies and universal life policies.

Whole Life Insurance

With whole life, an actuary in a back office has calculated what a person your age with your intended death benefit coverage, your health history, your potential lifespan—and other minutia—should pay for a premium rate. Depending on how the insurer's rate tables are calculated, your whole life policy will "endow" at a certain age—ninety, one hundred, one hundred twenty, etc.—so there is the risk you could outlive the policy, and the death benefit would pay out to you instead of your beneficiaries, which may create unplanned tax consequences.

Nonetheless, to qualify for your whole life policy, you will complete a medical questionnaire and possibly a paramedical exam, and then, based on that information, an underwriter will place you in one of these actuarial categories to determine your premium rate. One benefit of whole life insurance is the insurance company will credit a certain amount back into the policy's cash value based on your contract's guaranteed rate. Some insurance companies may also pay a dividend back to policyholders at the company's discretion.

Take Emma from the preceding example, and let's consider the scenario if her permanent insurance policy was a whole life policy. When she first purchased the contract, the insurance agent would have been able to tell her what her locked-in premium rate would be. She would pay the same amount, year after year, to keep her contract in force. And she could also calculate her policy's minimum cash value to the penny.

Universal Life Insurance

If whole life is the basic permanent life insurance policy, universal is the souped-up model. It has eight speeds, comes in many different colors, and has more options, which also means it might take some extra time and research to be thoroughly understood. But this means, if it's right for you, it can be even more customizable and fine-tuned to your specific needs.

The major differences:
- Flexible premium
- Increasing policy costs

Let's start with those increasing policy costs. Basically, the internal cost to the insurance company of maintaining your policy will increase over time, like a term insurance policy. Remember how whole life policies have those actuaries at the insurer's office calculating all of that and then determining a set rate for you to pay to cover it all? Well, with universal life, that's part of the flexible premium part. You can decide to pay a premium that will cover your future policy expenses, or you can decide to pay a premium that barely covers your current policy expenses, depending on your circumstances.

That is where these policies have gotten a bad rap in the past. If you purchase a policy and only ever pay the minimum premium required, your policy could end up losing value to the point your premium no longer covers your policy's expenses, and then the policy would lapse. That's also why it's incredibly important to work with a financial professional you trust, who can shoot straight about whether this kind of product would be appropriate for you and who makes sure you fully understand all the details.

To return to our example of Emma, though, here's how a well-set-up universal life insurance policy could work: Emma, ever the diligent saver, would have paid well over the minimum premium every month. Every time she got a raise or payroll increase, she increased the amount of premium she paid into her policy. With the policy's contractual rate of interest, she had a substantial amount of cash value accumulated in the policy. That way, when she decided to borrow money against the policy to help her brother, she could even afford to decrease her monthly payments for a time, until she was back in a better financial position.

Indexing

Now to the main event: *indexed* universal life insurance, or IUL. Like any permanent insurance, an IUL policy will remain in force as long as you continue to pay sufficient premiums, and you can borrow against your policy's cash value, income-tax-free. And, IUL policies are, at their core, universal life policies with that flexible premium. So, how are they different?

If you skim back through some of the other policy details, I covered the ability to withdraw the cash value of your policy without paying income taxes, even on the accumulation. Because of the index part of IULs, that accumulating cash value has the potential to accumulate more. An index is a tool that measures the movement of the market, like the S&P 500, or the Dow Jones Industrial Average. You can't invest directly in an index, it's just a sort of ruler.

With an IUL policy, your cash accumulation interest credits are based on an index, with what is called a "floor" and a "cap" or other limits such as a spread or participation rate. If the market does well, each year your policy can be credited interest on the cash accumulation based on whatever your policy's index is, subject to the cap, spread, or participation rate. If the market has a bad year and the index shows negative gains, your account still gets credited, whatever your contract floor is.

So, for example, let's say your contract cap is 12.5 percent and the floor is 0 percent. If the market returns 20 percent, your contract value gets a 12.5 percent interest credit. The next year, the S&P 500 returns a negative 26 percent. The insurance company won't credit your policy anything, but you also won't see your policy value slip because of that negative performance (although policy charges and expenses will still be deducted from your policy). So, your policy won't lose value because of poor market conditions, but you can still stand to realize interest credits due to changes in an index.

Another opportunity IUL presents is for a policyholder to overfund the policy cash value in the first five or ten years and then, potentially, not have to pay any more money into the policy, letting the cash accumulation self-fund the policy. However, when overfunding an IUL policy, it is important to understand the policy may become a modified endowment contract (or MEC) if premium payments exceed certain amounts specified under the Internal Revenue Code. This can happen if a policy has been funded too quickly in its early years. For MECs, distributions during the life of the insured (including loans) are fully taxable as income to the extent there is a gain in the policy over the amount of net premiums paid. An additional 10 percent federal income tax may apply for withdrawals made before age fifty-nine-and-one-half.

So, back to our friend, Emma. If her permanent life insurance policy was an IUL, what might that have looked like? Emma saves, paying well over the mandatory minimum of her IUL policy. Let's assume the market does well for decades. Her policy accumulates a significant cash value. At some point, she stops paying as much in premium, or maybe she stops paying any premium from her own pocket at all because her policy has enough in cash value it is paying for its own expenses with the insurance company. Then, when her brother needs help, there is enough cash value stored in the policy.

It's important to note that making withdrawals or taking policy loans from a policy may have an adverse effect. You may want to talk to your financial professional to re-evaluate your premium payment schedule if you are considering this option.

If you're reeling just a bit, it's understandable. There's a lot going on with these policies. If you don't take the time to understand the basics of how they work, it's entirely possible to fall behind on premium payments and end up with a policy that lapses. Yet, if you understand the terms of your contract and are working with purpose, an IUL could be a powerful cog in the greater mechanics of your overall retirement strategy.

IUL policies offer a guaranteed death benefit in a permanent cash value build-up policy that offers investment choices that index along with the stock market, but safely with no possible losses (like fixed indexed annuities—in fact, they're usually offered by the same insurance companies). These policies did not hit the scene until 1997. Just like any product in any industry, it takes a few years to saturate into the mainstream. The oldest IULs I have seen are from the early 2000s. The results I've seen have been very good. During the past twenty-year historically low-interest-rate environment, the IUL has performed exceptionally well. In fact, the typical quality IUL index account has outperformed its fixed indexed annuity brothers with almost identical indexing choices. This is because the typical life insurance company can structure the IUL indexing accounts more favorably in terms of how much interest the owner can earn inside the policy. That said, this is a life insurance policy and should be thought of in that context.

There are two main reasons I like IULs as opposed to other forms of cash value life insurance.

The first would be to provide a very cost-efficient permanent cash value life insurance policy with a high death benefit. The goal of the client here would be to purchase a permanent life insurance policy with the highest possible death benefit combined with the lowest initial premium necessary and a probability that no additional premiums would be due regardless of how old the policy got. IULs offer quite a bit of control to the owner compared to other life insurance products. You can control the amount of premium you want to pay, you can control the index investment choices inside the policy, and you can even adjust the death benefit down the road if you want to. Now, this comes with danger, because if the cash value buildup over the years has not been sufficient to keep pace with the internal cost of the life insurance, the client may be required to put in additional monies to prevent the policy from lapsing (lapsing = falling apart). But this is where we have historically seen IULs perform very well over the past twenty years. In my experience, if the clients paid the scheduled premiums from policy inception and the IUL was invested in a stock market-based index, the cash value growth has increased very well.

The second reason I like an IUL is for tax-free income for retirement. This especially works well if someone is ten years out or longer from wanting to start regular withdrawals. For some of our younger, very forward-thinking clients, finding out about an IUL early in the game can be a major tax game changer. I would first say that the client should want life insurance first and foremost to protect loved ones, but once that need is established, the IUL may offer a great income tax play for them.

Life insurance offers the owner the ability to take out principal as a withdrawal from cash value tax-free. Unlike other investments where withdrawals of value would be interest first (taxable), life insurance works just the opposite: principal first (tax-free). The reason principal is tax-free is that you've already paid tax on it. It is after-tax money. The special thing about life insurance is that the IRS allows you to take the principal out first. Beyond that, the owner is then able to take policy loans from the insurance company against the cash value. A loan is a non-taxable distribution of funds. If you were to get a mortgage to buy a house, there are no taxes on the funds the bank gives you. Those funds are tax-free. Can you imagine if the IRS started taxing loans? No one would buy anything. Eventually, the insured policy owner dies, and a portion of the death benefit goes back to the insurance company to pay off the loan in full, and "Poof!"—no income taxes are due because life insurance death benefits are income tax-free. The balance of the death benefit is paid to the named beneficiaries also tax-free. So, the IUL provides a strategy where the client could have tax-free income throughout retirement or maybe choose just to have additional tax-free income for a set period in retirement. This makes a ton of sense in a situation where the client was going to buy life insurance anyway to protect their family. Why not use those life insurance costs for something besides just the death benefit? Why not use it toward tax-free income in retirement?

Of course, all of this comes with stipulations.

First, you must qualify for the insurance. You don't just sign up for it. The good news here is that once you qualify, your health rating class is locked in the IUL permanently, even if your health gets poor later. The bad news is that we are all just a moment in time away from being diagnosed with something that will prevent us from ever getting new life insurance. So, the time to buy life insurance, if you think you need it, is now.

Then, unlike investments in your IRA or 401(k) or brokerage account, a life insurance policy has all sorts of life insurance costs being sucked out of it. Those costs are going to have a significant impact on the cash value accumulation over time. If the policy is being set up for anything beyond just the death benefit, like to have tax-free income, the client should have a thorough understanding of how the policy works. At the end of the day, if the cash value in the policy depletes to zero over time because the owner failed to pay the required premiums, took more in withdrawals/loans than the policy could handle, or had poor rates of return, the policy could run into trouble and even trigger a taxable event to the owner. The policy needs to be monitored by someone who knows what they're looking at, especially if withdraws or loans are being taken out of the account.

With that scary little statement, I will say my experience with my clients has been very positive with IUL. The cash value growth has performed as anticipated, and I have worked with several people who are using that cash value for tax-free income in retirement. The most common situation we have used it for is where a client wanted to retire early, like at fifty-five, but would not have access to their 401(k) and IRA retirement accounts until age fifty-nine and a half without IRS penalty. Life insurance has no limitations on age when it comes to withdrawal, so a fifty-five-year-old client could start taking out tax-free income for the beginning of their retirement and then switch over to the IRA or 401(k) withdrawals later after they were over age fifty-nine and a half. For that matter, a fifty-year-old could do the same thing.

Life insurance is just another tool. It may be low-cost term life insurance that makes the most sense for you right now just to protect your loved ones. If, however, you're looking for a cash value permanent life insurance policy, I do like the IUL best (compared to traditional universal life, whole life, variable universal life, or variable life) because it offers my client the most economical product and safe and secure cash value buildup. What this means in retirement is important: if a client is using it for tax-free income, the last thing they want to worry about is losing some of the cash value in the stock market combined with the cost of insurance fees being sucked out of that same cash value. You can't lose any cash value in an IUL due to stock market decline.

CHAPTER 10

Finding a Financial Professional

I wish I had a long, glorious story about my passion to become a financial advisor, but that is not the case. I graduated from college in 1990 with a B.A. in communications. I worked for an ABC Television affiliate broadcast station behind the camera producer (that is not nearly as glamorous as it sounds). One of my primary duties was to record the segment that still is used today on ABC's morning show, *Good Morning America*, where someone would say "Hi, this is so-and-so from middle of nowhere USA— good morning America!" We were responsible for filming anything within a 100-mile radius of our station. I liked the work I was doing, but like most young people, I discovered that it was probably not my long-term career path.

It was the opportunity of working with my dad and Uncle Marty that caused me to take a strong look at a financial services career. My dad knew I was having some second thoughts about a broadcasting career and mentioned to me that they would really like a relationship with a financial advisor they could trust. That's what led me down the Primrose Path. Thank God for small miracles!

I realized early on that financial planning is problem-solving, and that is pretty much what I had done back with ABC Television. Many times, we were off on a shoot and faced a situation where we had to think on our feet and problem-solve to get the job done. Those experiences carried over very well to how I help my clients today. I was led to a career of helping people with one of the most important parts of their life—money—and I love it.

I am a Registered Investment Adviser and fiduciary in the state of Illinois. This enables me to help individuals with fee-based written financial plans and fee-based investment management. I hold Series 6, Series 63, and Series 65 securities licenses.

I am also a registered life and health insurance broker in the state of Illinois. This enables me to help clients with fixed annuities and life insurance products. I have additional firm representatives who can help a client with other insurance products like Medicare Supplement insurance, long-term care insurance, disability insurance, or health insurance.

I received a B.A. in communications from Southern Illinois University in Carbondale, Illinois in 1990. In October 1992, I received my first financial services license: my Illinois life and health insurance license. In 1993, I received my Series 6 securities license, and in 2008, I became a Registered Investment Adviser with my Series 65 license.

For the first three years of my career from 1992 to 1995, I worked for Metropolitan life insurance company and their broker dealer, State Street securities. My experience at MetLife along with my veteran teachers, Ed Sr. the estate planning attorney and Uncle Marty the CPA, gave me a great foundation in proper financial planning for my clients. In 1996, I decided to become an independent representative to help clients with an unlimited array of financial products and services. In 2002, I founded Downey Financial Group, Inc. as a full-service independent firm offering financial planning, income planning, investment planning, tax planning, and estate and legacy planning.

Don't Go It Alone

Is it possible for you to do your own retirement income and tax planning? Of course it is. This is not rocket science. The financial concepts we help our clients understand are not complicated. In fact, I believe that over-complicating things is one of the biggest problems with my industry. We tend to make things way more complex than they actually are. I'm not sure what the intent is there, but it is not necessary.

However, although the concepts are not complicated, they are numerous. They are constantly changing. New ideas come out all the time. Laws change constantly. I have been doing this for thirty years and I still consider myself a student of the financial industry. Eight hours of my work week every week are devoted solely to ongoing education; two hours per day Monday through Thursday. Friday is my planning day, and I reserve it to complete Retirement Blueprints and keep up to date on the current financial environment. That's sixteen hours per week just studying and implementing financial concepts and investments. The rest of my work week is meeting with clients and perspective clients and my team.

So, the real question I have for you here is: Are you going to devote at least sixteen hours per week to manage your retirement income and tax plan? Maybe you don't need the full sixteen hours of research and implementation per week. I am managing 300-plus households and tens of millions of client dollars, and that is going to require more time than you. Maybe you only need ten hours per week, every week for the rest of your life. Does that fit in your calendar? No? Okay, how about five hours of solid dedicated focus time per week. Will that work? Two hours?

The reality is for most of the people reading this book the answer is zero hours. Most individuals do not want to do what it takes to properly administrate their retirement income and tax plans. Even for the few who do, unless they are a financial professional themselves, I question if they are really covering all the issues that need to be touched on for a thorough plan. I doubt it. Beyond my own thirty years of expertise, I rely on an entire team of professionals in various areas of expertise to alert me of different changes in the industry that I need to help my client with. There's no way I could do it by myself—I would miss things that were critical for my clients to know in a timely fashion. Therefore, I do not see how anyone can truly do it by themselves.

If you are going to go it on your own, you do need to start to create your own private team of professionals that you rely on to get you the information you need to make good decisions. You need to develop some type of system where you can be alerted when a financial crisis or opportunity presents itself. I believe working with a professional who you trust is a much easier and better path.

Most of the new clients I met back in the 1990s had a pension of some sort outside of their retirement investments. This pension on top of their Social Security covered the vast majority of what they needed to live on month by month and retirement. Very little of their retirement investments had to be used to supplement any income needed gap between pension and Social Security. This has changed for new clients I'm meeting today.

Unless they are a teacher or a government employee of some sort, most of my new clients do not have a pension. They have their Social Security and the retirement investments they worked so hard to save—and that's it. Statistically, Social Security will only cover about one-third of the income you are going to need to live on in retirement. This means that the vast majority, two-thirds of your income needs, must be generated on your own from your own retirement savings. All the risk of running out of money to live on is being taken up by you—the client. There is very little room for error; one bad decision could lead to financial ruin.

This is the biggest difference I see between today and thirty years ago for our clients. It is also why I believe financial planning is critical. You cannot invest your way through this. A very detailed and organized Retirement Blueprint needs to be created before any final decisions are made to develop the best outcome.

In many cases, we are doing multiple drafts of the Retirement Blueprint to see which one has the strongest probability of success.

What to Look for in a Professional

There are a few key things I would suggest you look for when hiring a financial professional. First and foremost, I would suggest you work with a Registered Investment Adviser (RIA). If you are working with an RIA, you are working with a fiduciary. Definition of fiduciary: "A fiduciary is someone who must legally put your interest first, even before his or her own interests; a fiduciary financial professional who is advising you about investments, must recommend investments that are best for you."[54]

Most RIAs are fee-only investment professionals. That means the way they make money is by charging you a fee for a set plan, or an hourly fee for advice, or charge a management fee based on asset value inside a brokerage account. They do not get paid commissions on investments the client purchases. What this means is that there is no bias on the RIA to have you in one investment or another as far as how much the advisor is earning. That is not how they are paid. They are compensated through a fee paid directly by the client. I believe this type of investment management structure makes the most sense for the client to get truly non-biased management and advice.

RIAs also can buy shares of funds at a discount for the client. For instance, let's say that you were interested in purchasing "A" share class of mutual fund "ABC"; its track record is great and the internal charges to manage the fund are very low compared to its competitors. However, there is an upfront load (sales commission charge) that you must pay when putting in new money. If instead the RIA purchases those same shares inside of a managed

---

[54] University of Illinois Extension. "Who Is a Fiduciary?"
https://web.extension.illinois.edu/financialpro/fiduciary.cfm

investment advisory account for you, the sales load is waived because the RIA cannot receive any commissions. Therefore, the client can invest in the "A" shares with the lower internal fees with no sales charge.

RIAs can also create written retirement income and tax plans for a fee. I believe having a written plan created by a professional is critical to making good decisions. If you are not paying someone a fee to guide your decision process, how are you going to make good decisions? Furthermore, how is that advisor being paid? Are they just hoping you'll buy something eventually?

I would also recommend you work with an advisor who offers insurance products as well as investment management. Life insurance, annuities, disability insurance, long-term care insurance, Medicare supplement insurance, etc. are critical tools needed to build your financial house properly. These products do pay the insurance agent a commission of some sort, but that commission is paid to the agent directly by the insurance company and does not come out of the client's pocket. Just be aware, though, that if you're buying an insurance product of some sort, someone is getting a commission somewhere for sure. Commissions can vary so that could create a bias for an agent to recommend one product over another. Be careful.

The last element I would recommend is that the advisor be independent. What independent means is that they are not an employee, franchisee, or subsidiary of some larger financial organization. I feel this is important for a couple of reasons.

The first would be to get truly non-biased advice. If you are working with an advisor who is not independent, they are going to be subject to the investments offered and approved by the firm. What if those approved offerings are not the best-in-class choices? What if the offerings are really best for the firm but not necessarily best for the client? That kind of setup automatically creates a bias. A good independent advisor on the other hand, like myself, has unlimited ability to get their clients all investments and products available to the public.

The second reason would be to get a fully comprehensive retirement income and tax plan. This would include a recommendation on taxes and estate planning. In many cases, that means that the financial advisor is going to recommend that the client talk to a CPA and an attorney, and probably ones that they know and work with. This makes non-independent firms nervous. What happens if that outside CPA or attorney does something wrong? What if their client decides to sue the outside CPA or attorney? Could the firm be implicated? They think all sorts of negative thoughts about the liability they may incur by referring a client to a CPA or attorney professional. It is very common for non-independent firms to discourage this type of referring. Independent firms on the other hand can make their own decisions about what makes sense for each client and may be more willing to introduce you to outside professionals they know and trust.

Warning Signs to Watch For

There are several red flags you should look out for in financial professionals:

Red flag #1: *They are not licensed to offer you security products or investment management.* More than likely, this would be an agent licensed only to sell insurance products. This is a real problem because the financial product toolbox available to the insurance-only agent is very limited. They only offer insurance company financial products; therefore, that is going to be what is recommended 100 percent of the time—probably an annuity of some sort. I consider them more financial salespeople instead of financial advisors. Be sure to ask the financial professional you are engaging with what their licenses are, and if they are securities licensed.

Red flag #2: *You are not invested in any exchange-traded funds (ETFs) in your portfolio with the advisor.* If you have a financial advisor who is managing a portfolio of mutual funds for you and not charging you an investment management fee, ask yourself "How are these people getting paid?" The answer to that question is that there may be a commission built into the mutual fund that pays the representative on an ongoing basis. This is called a trail commission. This fee is built-in to the entire expense of the fund and affects the share price every day, so it is a little hard for the client to see. You do not get a separate invoice or bill. But make no mistake, it's there and it is negatively affecting the performance of your mutual fund. That alone is not a problem. Everyone has to make a living. The problem here is that the representative is going to be paid that trail commission as long as you stay in the fund. That means there is no incentive for the representative to make suggestions to move OUT to another fund if in your best interest, especially if that new fund does not pay a trail commission! ETFs, on the other hand, do not pay any commissions of any kind to representatives. This prevents the advisor from having a possible commission conflict of interest in suggesting the best funds for the client. Please don't get me wrong—I am not anti-mutual fund. I would just say if you have a 100 percent mutual fund portfolio, you should ask your advisor why that is and how they are being compensated so you understand completely.

Red flag #3: *Your investment management professional does not have discretionary authority to manage your account.* If you have a registered representative or RIA managing your portfolio and you are paying them a management fee, you are either going to give them discretionary or non-discretionary trading authority. Discretionary trading authority means you permit the advisor to buy and sell securities for you, without having to contact you before every trade. This is done after you have acknowledged a good understanding of the portfolio investment philosophy. A non-discretionary authority means the advisor must contact you directly and talk to you live before any buy or sell trade is executed. My question is: how can a Registered Investment Advisor do their job properly on an ongoing daily basis without discretionary authority on your portfolio? The answer is: they can't. In my experience, most advisors have a non-discretionary relationship with the clients. Again, that means they must have permission from the client verbally before any trades. This is a real problem if you are expecting timely execution of opportunities that arise. Find out if your advisor has discretionary or non-discretionary authority on your portfolio. If it is non-discretionary, it could be because they do not want to take on the responsibility of having discretionary authority.

Red flag #4: *Your advisor does not bring up any tax planning for the current year or long-term.* This is a biggie. I have built a huge part of my practice on complete retirement income AND tax planning. Not having tax planning built-in would be the equivalent of a doctor saying he will treat the left side of your body but not the right. A lot of financial professionals are restricted from talking about tax planning by their corporate overlords. This again is why working with an independent financial advisor might be more productive. They don't have the restrictions that a captive non-independent advisor might have.

Downey Financial Group is an independent financial planning firm and has multiple CPA relationships offering a detailed multi-step approach to retirement tax planning for both our clients and our clients' beneficiaries. But I think a deeper reason why a lot of advisors don't talk tax is that they are just lazy. It takes a lot more work to explain and implement the tax planning. The advisor is going to earn the same asset management fee regardless of whether they get into tax planning with you. Why would they do the extra work? I charge a set planning fee that includes all the tax planning for our Retirement Blueprint clients.

Red flag #5: *Your advisor makes investment recommendations before a written retirement income and tax plan has been prepared.* "If you were going to build a brand-new house and you already owned the lot, what would be the first thing you would need to have prepared?" This is a question I ask every time I do a live workshop with new attendees. What do you think the number one response is? "The foundation!" is the top response. But it is not the correct answer. The correct answer is a blueprint.

The first thing you would need to have created by a professional once you had decided to build your new house and owned the land would be a blueprint. It is so interesting when I ask that question that "the foundation" is the number one response every time. I think it says something about our mentality about money. No planning. Just do. Imagine for a moment you were going to build a house and blew off hiring an architect to do a blueprint. Instead, you went to Home Depot and bought some shovels, rented a backhoe, got some bags of concrete, wood, conduit, and glass, and drove out to your lot and started digging in the ground. How do you think your house would turn out? Not too good. That may be a very good analogy for how your current retirement story looks. You need a detailed written understandable retirement income and tax plan that has every financial nut and bolt figured out before you act on anything. That's why we call ours the Retirement Blueprint.

You should also know how your financial advisor is being paid. Most of our new clients have no clue how their old advisor is being compensated. There is nothing wrong with making a living, but if your advisor has not had a conversation with you about how he or she is being paid, I would consider that a warning sign. The client should be very clear on how their advisor is being paid, how much, and whether there are breakpoints for the amount of assets being managed.

My Uncle Marty used to say, "It's not about how much you make, Eddie, it's how much you get to keep after taxes." Man, I just thought that was brilliant the first time I heard him say it. I found out later that it was an old saying that he had stolen from someone years earlier. Regardless, Uncle Marty gets the credit in my book, and it is one of the most important financial things I have ever learned. My experience with him was critical to my development in financial planning. He instilled the belief that a successful retirement plan has equal investment, income, and tax planning. Only doing one or two of these planning areas is an incomplete job.

I am a fan of the independent, smaller, family-run "mom and pop" type businesses. In my experience, successful small businesses like that thrive because they are very focused on the ultimate client experience. They can customize products and processes to their unique client's needs. This is one of the things Downey Financial Group clients have enjoyed over the years. We have been able to bring independent, non-biased advice and investments that are customizable to each household. This becomes more difficult for larger non-independent firms to achieve.

The goal of my company, and what we have posted on our website, is "To help people worry less about money." I discovered early in my career that many people are paralyzed with fear about running out of money. That fear causes them to make bad decisions, or even worse, no decisions at all (which is still a decision). Their situation gets even more dire when something bad happens like a market crash or large medical emergency, and that compounds the fear. I believe anxiety like this can easily create long-term medical problems for that individual. The sad part is most people will not seek professional financial advice due to skepticism, a belief they do not have a problem (even though they probably do and know it in their gut), or a negative experience with a financial salesperson in the past.

The good news is, I believe the odds of your situation being improvable through good planning is 99.99 percent. It is extremely rare I meet a potential client who I cannot help in some fashion. Our Retirement Blueprint software can show before and after planning scenarios, and the differences are often huge. It is my recommendation that you find a Registered Investment Adviser you trust and go through a detailed written retirement income and tax planning process that makes sense, and then act on the recommendations of that plan.

Fees

In recent years, advertising in your local newspaper has diminished. So too has the size of the paper. More people are accustomed to reading news online, or look for other sources, including those without a paywall. Advertisers don't find as much value in placing ads in the actual print version of the paper. Declines in circulation are to blame. Also, many former advertisers have company websites, which they use to drive consumer traffic.

However, if you happen to be someone who receives the newspaper in your driveway, you might have noticed that grocery store circulars are still a thing. Sure, the circulars might be a bit smaller. Yet, grocers still see some advantages to listing numerous prices for sales items in print, which readers can often scan much easier than looking up individual items on a website.

Those newspaper ads continue to be printed as a service to consumers. They want to see prices—in some cases before they ever step into the store—so they can prepare their shopping lists accordingly.

Why then should the cost of doing business with a financial professional often seem like a clandestine mystery? Well, to be blunt, it shouldn't. Consumers should know how much it will cost them to work with a financial professional and how exactly they arrive at the fees charged.

Now, fees can be troublesome. You can't get something for nothing, and fees are how many financial companies and professionals make a living. Yet, it's important to recognize even a fee of a single percentage point is money out of your pocket—money that represents not just the one-time fee of today but also represents an opportunity cost. For someone approaching retirement, how much do you think fees may have cost them over their lifetime?

It is important to look at management fees and assess if you think you're getting what you pay for. If you pay 1 percent in fees rather than 0.5 percent over a thirty-year period, you would have to save $2,156 more each year to finish with the same amount of savings in retirement.[55]

---

[55] Jean Folger. Investopedia. February 25, 2022. "Lower 401(k) Fees Mean More Money at Retirement." https://www.investopedia.com/how-to-lower-your-401-k-fees-4691479

About the Author

Edward F. Downey and Downey Financial Group, Inc.

As the president of Downey Financial Group, Ed is focused on helping clients work toward their retirement dreams through a well-thought-out strategy for retirement income.

Ed got his start in the industry in 1992, as a Registered Representative of State Street Securities and insurance agent at MetLife. He truly enjoys building retirement income and tax plans for individuals and watching their retirement dreams come to life.

Ed holds life and health insurance licenses in several states, with his resident state of Illinois Insurance License NPN: 2179753. Ed is also the owner and primary investment advisor of

DFG Wealth Management, LLC, a Registered Investment Advisory in the state of Illinois. He received a B.A. in communications from Southern Illinois University in Carbondale, Illinois in 1990.

Ed founded his independent firm, Downey Financial Group, in 2002. He is a Registered Investment Adviser and fiduciary in the state of Illinois. His firm has offered sound retirement income and tax planning suggestions for over twenty years. Over that time, Downey Financial Group has protected hundreds of families from over-taxation and extreme market downturns and provided clients with a path for retirement that makes sense.

Beyond planning, Ed's firm has helped clients with their tax preparation. Since 2002, the firm has prepared thousands of tax returns. Ed says, "I don't know how an advisor does proper tax planning if he is not deeply involved in the preparation and review of the client's actual tax return."

Ed was born and raised in Chicagoland, is blessed to have a great wife plus three awesome kids, and has lived in the Western Suburbs for over twenty years.

You can reach Downey Financial Group Inc. at:
806 W. Bartlett Road
Bartlett, IL 60103
(630) 233-6060
www.DowneyFG.com

Acknowledgements

There are a few key people I want to thank who made this book possible. The first is my former new business and service administrator, Karen Alwin. She was one of the first staff members I hired back in 2003 and worked with me for seventeen years until her retirement in 2020. Through good times and bad, Karen was completely dedicated to the success of Downey Financial Group and our clients. Her hard work and professionalism made a huge difference with the credibility of our firm. Thank you, Karen.

The second person is the Chief Strategy Officer at Advisors Excel, Matt Neuman. Matt and I have known each other since 2010 and he has been instrumental in the growth of Downey Financial Group, and me as an advisor. From early in our relationship, Matt suggested that I write about what we do for our clients. It was his confidence in me and coaching that enabled me to write this book. Thank you, Matt.

The last person, and by far the most important, is my wife, Shannon Downey. They say the most important decision you will make is who you decide to marry. Well, I got super lucky in that department. Ever since I met Shannon, she has supported me in every way possible. She has been there with emotional support during rough times, and helped celebrate the big accomplishments. She has been our backup employee who dropped everything else she had going whenever we needed her to come in and help. Thank you, Shannon. I love you very much.

Made in the USA
Columbia, SC
28 September 2022